BENEFITS REALIZATION MANAGEMENT: A PRACTICE GUIDE

Library of Congress Cataloging-in-Publication Data

Names: Project Management Institute, publisher.
Title: Benefits realization management : a practice guide.
Description: Newtown Square : Project Management Institute, 2018. | Includes
  bibliographical references and index.
Identifiers: LCCN 2018053717 (print) | LCCN 2018058018 (ebook) | ISBN
  9781628254815 (ePub) | ISBN 9781628254822 (kindle) | ISBN 9781628254839
  (Web PDF) | ISBN 9781628254808 (paperback)
Subjects: LCSH: Project management. | Project management--Cost effectiveness.
  | Strategic planning. | BISAC: BUSINESS & ECONOMICS / Project Management.
  | BUSINESS & ECONOMICS / Strategic Planning.
Classification: LCC HD69.P75 (ebook) | LCC HD69.P75 B4476 2018 (print) | DDC
  658.4/04--dc23
LC record available at https://lccn.loc.gov/2018053717

ISBN: 978-1-62825-480-8

Published by:
  Project Management Institute, Inc.
  14 Campus Boulevard
  Newtown Square, Pennsylvania 19073-3299 USA
  Phone: +610-356-4600
  Fax: +610-356-4647
  Email: customercare@pmi.org
  Internet: www.PMI.org

©2019 Project Management Institute, Inc. All rights reserved.

Our copyright content is protected by U.S. intellectual property law that is recognized by most countries. To republish or reproduce our content, you must obtain our permission. Please go to http://www.pmi.org/permissions for details.

To place a Trade Order or for pricing information, please contact Independent Publishers Group:
  Independent Publishers Group
  Order Department
  814 North Franklin Street
  Chicago, IL 60610 USA
  Phone: +1 800-888-4741
  Fax: +1 312-337-5985
  Email: orders@ipgbook.com (For orders only)

For all other inquiries, please contact the PMI Book Service Center.
  PMI Book Service Center
  P.O. Box 932683, Atlanta, GA 31193-2683 USA
  Phone: 1-866-276-4764 (within the U.S. or Canada) or +1-770-280-4129 (globally)
  Fax: +1-770-280-4113
  Email: info@bookorders.pmi.org

Printed in the United States of America. No part of this work may be reproduced or transmitted in any form or by any means, electronic, manual, photocopying, recording, or by any information storage and retrieval system, without prior written permission of the publisher.

The paper used in this book complies with the Permanent Paper Standard issued by the National Information Standards Organization (Z39.48—1984).

PMI, the PMI logo, PMBOK, OPM3, PMP, CAPM, PgMP, PfMP, PMI-RMP, PMI-SP, PMI-ACP, PMI-PBA, PROJECT MANAGEMENT JOURNAL, PM NETWORK, PMI TODAY, PULSE OF THE PROFESSION and the slogan MAKING PROJECT MANAGEMENT INDISPENSABLE FOR BUSINESS RESULTS. are all marks of Project Management Institute, Inc. For a comprehensive list of PMI trademarks, contact the PMI Legal Department. All other trademarks, service marks, trade names, trade dress, product names and logos appearing herein are the property of their respective owners. Any rights not expressly granted herein are reserved.

10 9 8 7 6 5 4 3

NOTICE

The Project Management Institute, Inc. (PMI) standards and guideline publications, of which the document contained herein is one, are developed through a voluntary consensus standards development process. This process brings together volunteers and/or seeks out the views of persons who have an interest in the topic covered by this publication. While PMI administers the process and establishes rules to promote fairness in the development of consensus, it does not write the document and it does not independently test, evaluate, or verify the accuracy or completeness of any information or the soundness of any judgments contained in its standards and guideline publications.

PMI disclaims liability for any personal injury, property or other damages of any nature whatsoever, whether special, indirect, consequential or compensatory, directly or indirectly resulting from the publication, use of application, or reliance on this document. PMI disclaims and makes no guaranty or warranty, expressed or implied, as to the accuracy or completeness of any information published herein, and disclaims and makes no warranty that the information in this document will fulfill any of your particular purposes or needs. PMI does not undertake to guarantee the performance of any individual manufacturer or seller's products or services by virtue of this standard or guide.

In publishing and making this document available, PMI is not undertaking to render professional or other services for or on behalf of any person or entity, nor is PMI undertaking to perform any duty owed by any person or entity to someone else. Anyone using this document should rely on his or her own independent judgment or, as appropriate, seek the advice of a competent professional in determining the exercise of reasonable care in any given circumstances. Information and other standards on the topic covered by this publication may be available from other sources, which the user may wish to consult for additional views or information not covered by this publication.

PMI has no power, nor does it undertake to police or enforce compliance with the contents of this document. PMI does not certify, test, or inspect products, designs, or installations for safety or health purposes. Any certification or other statement of compliance with any health or safety-related information in this document shall not be attributable to PMI and is solely the responsibility of the certifier or maker of the statement.

TABLE OF CONTENTS

1. INTRODUCTION 1
   1.1 Purpose 1
   1.2 Need for BRM 2
   1.3 Intended Audience 4
   1.4 Overview of Content 5
2. BRM AND ORGANIZATIONAL CONTEXT 7
   2.1 Overview 7
   2.2 Organizational Strategy and Benefits 9
      2.2.1 Connecting Business Strategy to BRM 10
      2.2.2 Organizational Goals as Drivers 11
      2.2.3 Sponsorship and Benefits 12
   2.3 BRM Core Principles 12
      2.3.1 Net Benefits Justify the Use of Invested Resources 13
      2.3.2 Commencement of Work Is Driven by Benefits Identification 13
      2.3.3 Planned Benefits Are Identified in Authorizing Documents 13
      2.3.4 Benefits Realization Is Holistically Planned and Managed 14
      2.3.5 Governance and Adequate Resources Are Essential to BRM Success ... 14
   2.4 BRM Critical Success Enablers 14
      2.4.1 Establish Clear BRM Roles and Responsibilities 15
      2.4.2 Develop the Right BRM Culture 15
      2.4.3 Build the Right Skill Sets 16
      2.4.4 Embrace Flexibility 18
      2.4.5 Strengthen Governance and Risk Management 19
      2.4.6 Establish Benefits Tracking 19

2.5 Organizational BRM Roles and Responsibilities 20
2.5.1 Organizational Strategy and Sponsorship 21
2.5.2 Portfolio Roles and BRM 22
2.5.3 Program Roles and BRM 23
2.5.4 Project Roles and BRM 24

3. BRM FRAMEWORK 25
3.1 Overview 27
3.2 Identify Stage 27
3.2.1 Develop Business Case and Benefits Realization Management Plan 28
3.2.2 Authorize Charter 28
3.3 Execute Stage 29
3.3.1 Develop Outputs 30
3.3.2 Deliver Outputs and Transfer Ownership of Outputs to Realize Benefits 30
3.4 Sustain Stage 31
3.4.1 Realize-Sustain Benefits 31
3.4.2 Adapt Benefits 32
3.5 Supporting Practices Across the BRM Life Cycle 32
3.5.1 Key Interactions 32
3.5.2 Principal Supporting BRM Tools 33
3.5.3 Categorizing Benefits 37
3.5.3.1 Common Categories of Benefits 38
3.5.3.2 Additional Categorization 40
3.5.4 Benefits Measurement 41
3.5.4.1 Factors Influencing Benefits Measurement 42
3.5.4.2 Roles and Benefits Measurement 46
3.5.4.3 Timing of Benefits Measurement 46
3.5.5 Benefits and Requirement Traceability 46

4. GUIDANCE FOR PORTFOLIO, PROGRAM, AND PROJECT MANAGEMENT IN A BRM CONTEXT 51

4.1 Overview 51
4.2 BRM General Guidance for Portfolio Managers 53
4.3 BRM General Guidance for Program Managers 54
4.4 BRM General Guidance for Project Managers 55
4.5 BRM General Guidance for Business Analysts 56

APPENDIX X1
CONTRIBUTORS AND REVIEWERS OF
BENEFITS REALIZATION MANAGEMENT: A PRACTICE GUIDE 57

X1.1 BRM Core Committee 57
X1.2 SME Reviewers 58
X1.3 PMI Standards Program Member Advisory Group (MAG) 58
X1.4 Production Staff 59

APPENDIX X2
BENEFITS REALIZATION MANAGEMENT READINESS SURVEY 61

X2.1 Core Principles of BRM 62
X2.1.1 Net Benefits Justify the Use of Invested Resources (Table X2-1) 62
X2.1.2 Commencement of Work Is Driven by Benefits Identification (Table X2-2) 63
X2.1.3 Planned Benefits Are Identified in Authorizing Documents (Table X2-3) 63
X2.1.4 Benefits Realization Is Holistically Planned and Managed (Table X2-4) 64
X2.1.5 Governance and Adequate Resources Are Essential to BRM Success (Table X2-5) 65

 X2.2 BRM Critical Success Enablers (CSEs) 65
  X2.2.1 Establish Clear BRM Roles and Responsibilities (Table X2-6) 65
  X2.2.2 Develop the Right BRM Culture (Table X2-7) 66
  X2.2.3 Build the Right Skill Sets (Table X2-8) 68
  X2.2.4 Embrace Flexibility (Table X2-9) 70
  X2.2.5 Strengthen Governance and Risk Management (Table X2-10) 70
  X2.2.6 Establish Benefits Tracking (Table X2-11) 71

APPENDIX X3
BRM RESEARCH SUMMARY 73
 X3.1 Report #1 73
  X3.1.1 Purpose of Report #1 73
  X3.1.2 Findings and Reflections from Report #1 74
  X3.1.3 Conclusion and Recommendations from Report #1 74
 X3.2 Report #2 76
  X3.2.1 Purpose of Report #2 76
  X3.2.2 Conclusion and Recommendations from Report #2 78

REFERENCES 79

BIBLIOGRAPHY 81

GLOSSARY 85

INDEX 89

LIST OF TABLES AND FIGURES

Figure 2-1. The Benefits-Value Equation 8
Figure 2-2. Connecting Organizational Strategy to BRM 9
Figure 2-3. Examples of Benefits that Organizations May Realize 11
Figure 2-4. BRM Sphere of Influence and Roles 20
Figure 3-1. BRM Framework in the Context of Portfolios, Programs, and Projects 26
Figure 3-2. Benefits Realization Management Plan Concept 29
Figure 3-3. Example Benefit Profile 34
Figure 3-4. Benefits Register 35
Figure 3-5. Example Benefits Map 36
Figure 3-6. Benefits Traceability Matrix 37
Figure 3-7. Benefits Categorization Cube 39
Figure 3-8. Example of Value Driver Map to Help Identify and Plan Benefits 48
Figure 4-1. Portfolio-Program and Project Life Cycles in BRM Context 52

Table 2-1. Typical Organizational Strategic Roles and Responsibilities in BRM 21
Table 2-2. Typical Portfolio Roles and Responsibilities in BRM 22
Table 2-3. Typical Program Roles and Responsibilities in BRM 23
Table 2-4. Typical Project Roles and Responsibilities in BRM 24
Table 3-1. Brief Example of Benefit Measurements 44
Table 3-2. Example Configuration of Benefits Measurement Resource 45

Table X2-1.	Principle: Net Benefits Justify the Use of Invested Resources	62
Table X2-2.	Principle: Commencement of Work Is Driven by Benefits Identification	63
Table X2-3.	Principle: Planned Benefits Are Identified in Authorizing Documents	64
Table X2-4.	Principle: Benefits Realization Is Holistically Planned and Managed	64
Table X2-5.	Principle: Governance and Adequate Resources Are Essential to BRM Success	65
Table X2-6.	CSE: Clear BRM Roles and Responsibilities Are Established	66
Table X2-7.	CSE: Right BRM Culture Is Developed	67
Table X2-8.	CSE: The Right Skill Sets Are Developed	69
Table X2-9.	CSE: Flexibility Is Embraced	70
Table X2-10.	CSE: Governance and Risk Management Are Strengthened	71
Table X2-11.	CSE: Benefits Tracking Established	71
Table X3-1.	Summary of Report #1 Research Findings	75
Table X3-2.	Report #1 Recommendations	76
Table X3-3.	Summary of Report #2 Research Findings	77
Table X3-4.	Report #2 Recommendations	78

PREFACE

The concept of portfolios, programs, and projects delivering value through benefits realization management (BRM) can be traced back to the logical framework approach (LFA), developed in 1969 for the U.S. Agency for International Development. LFA is a methodology mainly used for designing, monitoring, and evaluating international development projects. In the private sector, BRM arose in the information technology (IT) industry about 30 years ago when the evolution of this technology made it more important that investments in planned benefits came to fruition. The practice of BRM has since proved useful to other industries where benefits derive from portfolio, program, and project outputs. Although there is no widespread consensus on BRM as a discipline, it continues to evolve and be recognized as a useful management approach.

Significant drivers of this evolution are:

◆ Increased business focus on the ability to accommodate rapid change;

◆ New and evolving benefits management approaches to deliver planned outcomes and benefits that drive value; and,

◆ A long-standing need to link outputs of portfolios, programs, and projects to results, benefits, and value as efficiently and effectively as possible.

With these considerations, *Benefits Realization Management: A Practice Guide* offers practitioners an aggregation of current BRM concepts and approaches for engaging BRM effectively. It provides guidance on BRM practices within organizations that use portfolios, programs, and projects, and is intended to support and complement PMI's foundational standards to help drive successful business outcomes.

This new practice guide provides:

◆ A diverse collection of both long-established and recent concepts and practices, defined and explained by experienced BRM practitioners; and,

◆ General guidance on how these concepts and practices could be used to improve the effectiveness of BRM.

1

INTRODUCTION

1.1 PURPOSE

This practice guide describes benefits realization management (BRM) with a focus on products, services, results, or process improvement. BRM covers the day-to-day organization and management of the effort to achieve and sustain potential benefits arising from investments in portfolios, programs, and projects. BRM presents knowledge needed to conduct BRM regardless of the benefit's focus.

This practice guide:

- Provides a practical description of what BRM is;
- Defines the role and life cycle relationships of BRM to portfolios, programs, and projects;
- Describes why BRM is important;
- Identifies the key principles and critical success enablers needed to help an organization achieve the realization of planned benefits they seek as part of its strategic vision;
- Provides general guidance for organizations in establishing their approach to BRM in the context of portfolios, programs, projects, and organizational change management; and
- Identifies a common vocabulary to aid in the discussion of BRM.

In addition, this practice guide is intended to help practitioners to:

- Understand the fundamentals of BRM,
- Consider how to adapt and adjust existing techniques and practices to meet organizational needs, and,
- Support BRM in areas of practice where there may not yet be consensus as to how BRM should be used or changed for the better.

The choice of BRM practices—and how organizations tailor what they choose to implement—is highly dependent on organizational, cultural, and practice norms. This practice guide aims to help practitioners better understand what it means to actively manage benefits as an integral part of portfolio, program, and project management thinking, activities, responsibilities, and accountabilities.

The information and guidelines in this practice guide may be used in whole or in part to develop manual or automated practices with any type of strategic management, including portfolio, program, and project life cycles that the organization uses.

1.2 NEED FOR BRM

Facing rapid change and increasing complexity, organizations struggle to implement the strategies they need to generate and sustain a competitive advantage. There is a greater need now than ever before to ensure that the investments in portfolios, programs, and projects lead to clear, sustainable benefits. A benefit is defined as a gain realized by the organization and beneficiaries through portfolio, program, or project outputs and resulting outcomes.

There is often a gap in the appropriate tracking from planned to actual realization of benefits. BRM is an approach used to close that gap, by aligning portfolios, programs, and projects to the organization's overarching strategy. Good BRM helps correct strategy misalignment, improve initiatives selection, integrate outputs and outcomes, and transition to operations resulting in measurable benefits that deliver more value to the organization. Value is defined as the net result of realized benefits less the cost of achieving these benefits. According to a survey conducted by the Project Management Institute (PMI) in its *2018 Pulse of the Profession® Report: Success in Disruptive Times* [1]:[1]

- ◆ Fewer than 1 in 10 organizations report having a very high maturity with their value delivery capabilities.
- ◆ The average percentage of projects that met original goals/business intent was 78% for mature organizations and 56% for immature organizations.
- ◆ Only 31% of organizations are prioritizing the development of a comprehensive value delivery capability.
- ◆ Of the champion companies, those making the investment to have high-delivery capabilities, 87% report having achieved high-delivery capabilities versus only 5% for underperformers.

---

[1] The numbers in brackets refer to the list of references at the end of this practice guide.

Establishing formal or improving existing BRM processes requires focusing on several priorities:

◆ Managing portfolios of programs and projects based on planned strategic outcomes and benefits—and, specifically, value creation for the organization;

◆ Recognizing the extent of organizational change required if planned benefits are to be realized;

◆ Creating an environment for regular dialogue to secure alignment, assess progress, and course-correct, as needed, right from the start of each initiative among:

- Highest-level executives,
- Organization owners,
- Senior end users, and
- Appropriate portfolio, program, and project managers; and

◆ Establishing the right conditions for success, including:

- Setting expectations regarding the key principles of BRM,
- Establishing the supporting behaviors for those principles,
- Fostering a value-oriented environment, and
- Having the right portfolio, program, and project managers in place, along with senior-level leadership committed to doing BRM well.

BRM is a continuous journey in which organizations learn by doing and improving their performance over time. Organizations can advance BRM capabilities significantly through incremental steps, for example, launching multiple quick-win measures to build up experience rapidly.

PMI research reinforces the value-add role of portfolio, program, and project management in BRM. However, the research also shows that levels of responsibility and accountability vary in practice, especially for proactively managing BRM with monitoring and reporting metrics and other critical information, such as progress measurement against the benefits realization management plan.

Not surprisingly, fewer than half of the surveyed organizations identify any role for project managers to help ensure that the planned benefits realized through a project's deliverables are aligned and stay aligned, with the strategic goals and objectives associated with the portfolio/program of which the project is a part. Together with portfolio and program managers, project managers can fill a useful role in helping ensure benefits are realized by the intended beneficiary. In a mature BRM environment, the responsibility for the strategic alignment of projects within a given program belongs to the program manager, and the strategic alignment of programs and nonprogram projects resides with the portfolio manager and benefit owner(s).

While this finding further illustrates how many executive leaders do not fully connect portfolio, program, and project management with achieving strategic objectives, it also highlights that BRM is a shared responsibility among portfolio, program, and project managers, benefit owners, organization owners, executive sponsors (sometimes known as senior responsible owners), and other senior leaders.

This practice guide provides a resource to help organizations and practitioners successfully achieve the realization of planned benefits from critical initiatives. However, it is recognized that not all organizations manage temporary work using all three domains of portfolio, program, and project management. Still, these organizations should benefit by adapting the principles and practices of BRM to fit the organization's needs. For example, when an organization does not practice formal portfolio management but only implements initiatives by projects, as in many small-to-medium entities, project managers should interface directly with the senior leaders responsible for the planned benefits that the project outcomes are expected to generate.

1.3 INTENDED AUDIENCE

This practice guide is intended for anyone who is responsible for:

- Identifying and achieving benefits expected from investments in portfolios, programs, and projects;
- Communicating benefits-related issues with executives and/or sponsors;
- Ensuring planned benefits stay aligned with and contribute to an organization's strategic goals and objectives; and
- Ensuring benefits that accrue from the outputs of portfolios, programs, and projects are realized and sustained.

Included in this group are, but not limited to:

- Benefit owners,
- Senior end users,
- Executive management team,
- Executive sponsors,
- Portfolio and program management office (PMO) managers,
- Functional/operations managers,
- Organizational change managers,

- Business analysts, and
- Portfolio, program, and project managers and their respective team members.

This practice guide has been developed to help practitioners obtain improvements in overall competency levels and in the application of BRM in portfolio, program, and project environments.

1.4 OVERVIEW OF CONTENT

This practice guide is organized as follows:

- **Section 1 Introduction.** This section includes an overview of the purpose and need for publishing PMI's first practice guide on BRM. The rationale and intended audience for this guide are also defined.

- **Section 2 BRM and Organizational Context.** This section describes where BRM fits in the organization, how strategy relates to benefits, what the core principles and critical success enablers of BRM are, along with a summary of organizational BRM roles and responsibilities.

- **Section 3 BRM Framework Overview.** This section describes the Identify, Execute, and Sustain life-cycle stages and the supporting activities, practices, and common tools needed to provide a viable BRM system in conjunction with the organization's portfolios, program, and projects.

- **Section 4 Guidance for Portfolio, Program, and Project Managers in a BRM Context.** This section offers guidance to portfolio, program, and project managers, as well as business analysts, on what actions and practices support and enhance engagement of their respective domains with BRM life-cycle activities.

- **Appendix X1 Contributors and Reviewers of** *Benefits Realization Management: A Practice Guide*.

- **Appendix X2 Benefits Realization Management Readiness Survey.**

- **Appendix X3 BRM Research Summary.**

- **Glossary.** The glossary provides definitions of key BRM terms.

2

BRM AND ORGANIZATIONAL CONTEXT

This section describes foundational terms, concepts, principles, critical success enablers, and roles and responsibilities. In addition, it gives an overview on the topics of organizational strategy and benefits, benefits and requirements traceability, benefits categorization considerations, and benefits measurement.

2.1 OVERVIEW

BRM encompasses the standard methods and processes that an organization uses for identifying benefits, executing its benefits realization management plans, and sustaining the realized benefits facilitated by portfolio, program, and project initiatives. BRM requires alignment with an organization's strategy, a solid understanding of key principles, and techniques as described in this chapter.

The terms *benefit* and *value* are often used interchangeably. However, it is important to understand their differences and the direct relationship between benefits and portfolios, programs, and projects. In this practice guide, a *benefit* is defined as a gain realized by the organization and beneficiaries through portfolio, program, or project outputs and resulting outcomes. *Value*, however, is the net result of realized benefits less the cost of achieving these benefits. Value may be tangible or intangible. Figure 2-1 illustrates this equation.

Cost management is extensively described in *A Guide to the Project Management Body of Knowledge (PMBOK® Guide)* [2] and the *Practice Standard for Earned Value Management* [3]. The focus on BRM is on the benefits component of Figure 2-1, including tangible and intangible benefits (see Section 3.5.3 for a discussion on tangible and intangible benefits). Quantifying benefits and allocating appropriate costs for attaining these benefits can be difficult in some cases due to the degree of subjectivity involved. This can be especially true when quantifying intangible benefits, although there are methods that aid in quantifying intangible benefits such as the use of proxy or representative measures.

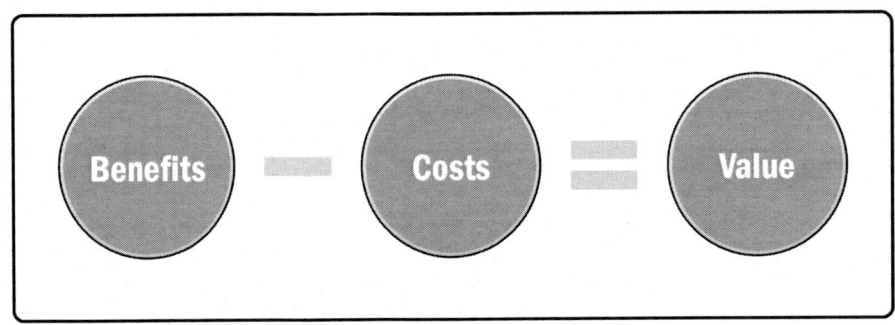

Figure 2-1. The Benefits-Value Equation

For example, the value of a better customer experience (an intangible benefit) achieved through a new website with an artificial intelligence (AI) engine (a project output) can be valued in monetary terms through increased sales through the website (a representative or substitute tangible measure) less the cost of implementing the AI project.

Benefits realization is the intended beneficiaries' integration of gains resulting from the use of outputs of portfolios, programs, and projects. The need for the integration of these gains and the resulting value to the organization serves to drive organizations to pursue more effective BRM practices. Time and measurement horizons are important factors in the assessment, planning, realization, and measurement of benefits, costs, and resulting value as they vary over time. Benefits realization management is the day-to-day organization and management of the effort to achieve and sustain planned benefits arising from investment in portfolios, programs, and projects.

Since benefits are "gains realized by the organization and beneficiaries," this implies that benefits are the positive outcomes or the results of an organizational investment. When organizations set their strategic goals and organizational objectives, each are coupled with planned benefits. These benefits have a beginning and sustainment period and are managed throughout their respective life cycles. (Section 3 describes the BRM framework, life cycle, and related practices.)

Executives are responsible for driving organizations forward, by setting goals and objectives by means of an organizational strategic plan. The objectives of the organizational strategy are then decomposed into initiatives (portfolios, programs, and projects), which deliver outputs that collectively become outcomes and, ultimately, realize benefits.

The primary purpose of managing portfolios is to choose the appropriate set of programs and projects and execute them to realize the planned benefits and optimize organizational value. For organizations that do not engage in portfolio or program management but carryout initiatives by using project management practices, the challenge is still the same—the organization chooses the appropriate set of projects and executes them effectively to realize the planned benefits.

The process of managing benefits spans the time before an initiative officially starts, during the time in which it is executed, and after the initiative has been completed carrying through the benefits sustainment period during which benefits accumulate and are being realized. It is important that roles and responsibilities (see Section 2.5) are declared once the strategy has been agreed upon. It is equally important that the characteristics of goals, objectives, and related benefits are clearly understood and agreed by the business stakeholders. Techniques such as the use of RACI charts are a common approach used to ensure clarity around roles and responsibilities for benefits realization.

2.2 ORGANIZATIONAL STRATEGY AND BENEFITS

Organizations develop visions, missions, and strategies to guide their direction. Those strategies are tied to larger, overarching goals that have associated benefits. For example, a city may have a strategic objective to improve the local economy. Some associated benefits of that strategic objective could be increased revenue from tourism, more jobs, and more attractions/facilities. Goals are then decomposed into organizational objectives that are executed via portfolio, program, and project management initiatives to deliver outputs, which result in outcomes. The outcomes then yield planned benefits that ultimately deliver the value sought by the organization. Figure 2-2 provides an overview of how strategy is linked to the initiatives of portfolios, programs, and projects to deliver outputs. The outputs result in outcomes, which yield benefits and, ultimately, organizational value.

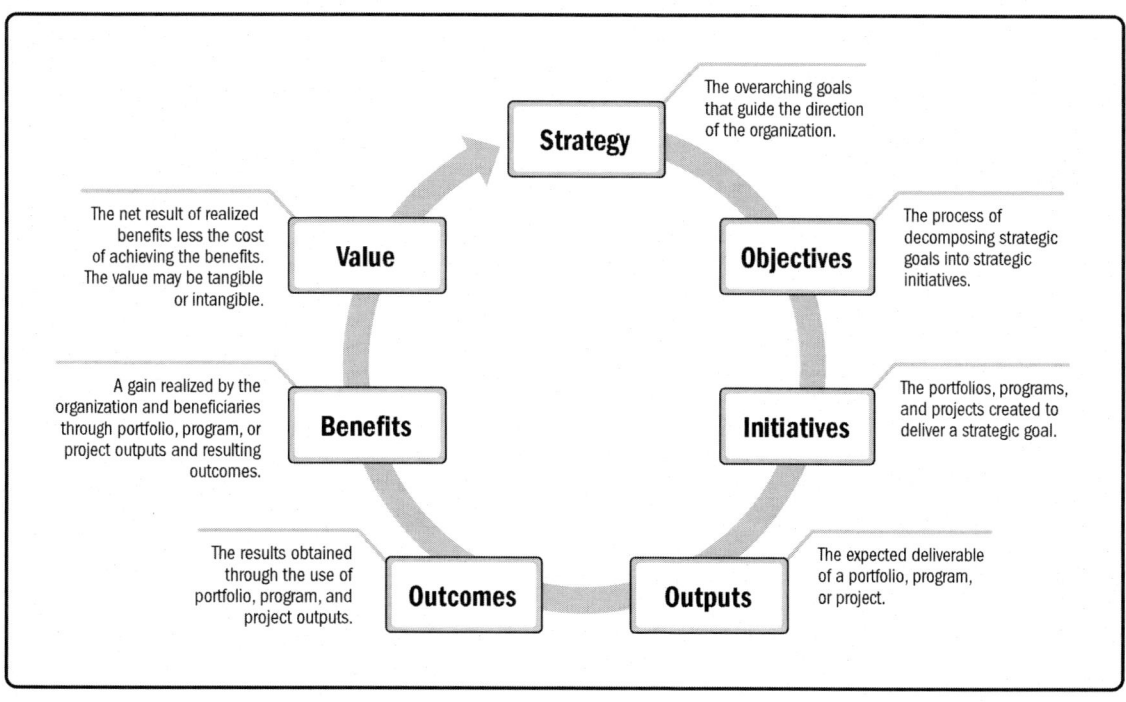

Figure 2-2. Connecting Organizational Strategy to BRM

Portfolios, programs, and projects are created to achieve strategic goals and realize the associated benefits being sought as part of organizational strategy. The management of benefits occurs throughout the organization's strategic life cycle.

Similar to enterprise environmental factors outlined in the *PMBOK® Guide*, external drivers are factors outside of the organization's control that influence or dictate the strategy or direction of an organization. In the context of BRM, external drivers can influence which goals are seen as relevant to the organization's overall strategy as it pertains to delivering the planned intended benefits. External drivers are a necessary consideration for developing organizational strategies, which ultimately may determine the probability of realizing the planned benefits.

Some examples of external drivers that influence goals and, therefore, benefits realization include:

◆ Competitive landscape, for example, goals to maintain or create a competitive advantage;

◆ Innovation, for example, the need to advance technologically to encourage relevance;

◆ Political influences, for example, changes to the political landscape that impact the way the organization operates or competes;

◆ Customer needs, for example, the need for more efficient or automated ways of doing things;

◆ Economic, for example, a sudden change in the price of a commodity that the organization uses;

◆ Regulatory decisions, for example, reflections of legislative policy and intent that significantly alter ways of doing business; and

◆ Cultural preferences of external stakeholders and beneficiaries.

2.2.1 CONNECTING BUSINESS STRATEGY TO BRM

At the organizational strategy and portfolio levels, benefits should be closely aligned to strategic goals and organizational objectives. As shown in Figure 2-3, there are many types of benefits an organization may seek as part of pursuing its strategic goals and organizational objectives [4].

The organization's benefits management realization strategy lays out its high-level direction for managing planned benefits achieved through portfolio, program, and project outputs.

Organizations develop a benefits realization management plan providing a documented explanation of the organization's planned activities, timeframes, and criteria for achieving one or more planned benefits or a group of related benefits. This provides a broad view of how the organization plans to address benefits management.

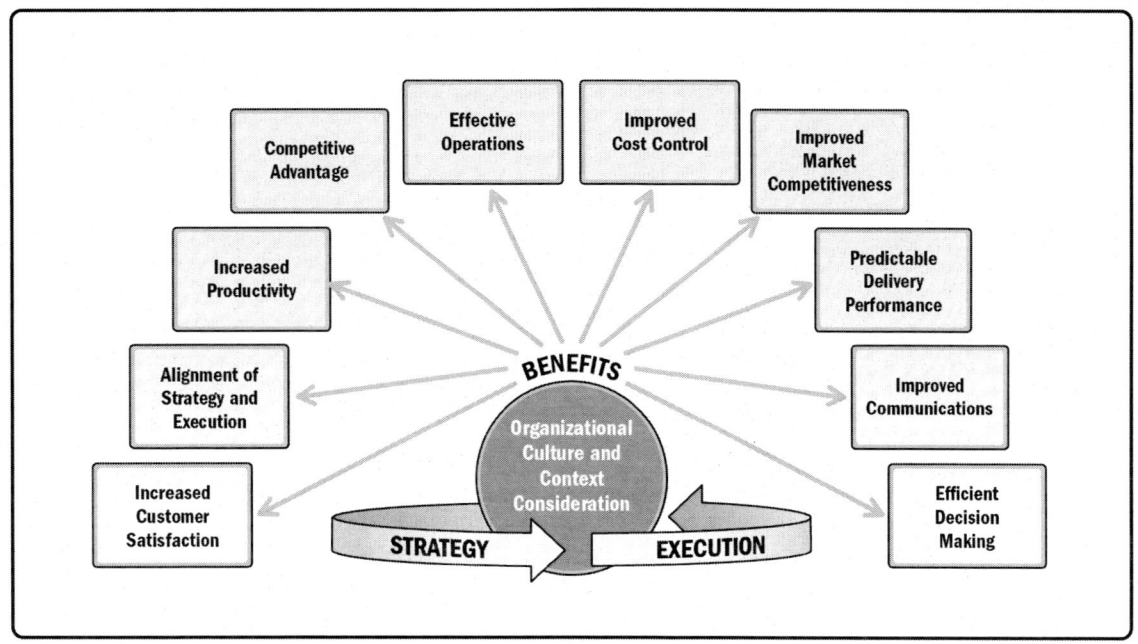

Figure 2-3. Examples of Benefits that Organizations May Realize

As planned benefits are identified and aligned to their respective organizational objectives and associated portfolio, program, or project initiatives, tools such as benefit maps, benefit profiles, benefits registers, and benefits traceability matrices can be used to further describe the benefits (see Section 3.5.2). These tools help capture the planned benefits and their associated attributes. The tools also provide a means to trace the benefits back to the strategic goals and organizational objectives and other planned initiatives aimed at generating these benefits.

2.2.2 ORGANIZATIONAL GOALS AS DRIVERS

Organizational goals contain objectives that outline how they are to be achieved. The organization's strategic direction and goals subsequently drive the expected gains (benefits) as depicted in Figure 2-2.

The ties between strategy, goals, and benefits are interconnected. Special care should be taken to ensure goals and planned benefits are aligned. This alignment can be facilitated using a benefits register and benefits traceability matrix.

When organizations consider commissioning portfolios, programs, or projects, various factors (e.g., strategic fit and market conditions) impact their decisions whether to proceed with these initiatives. Planned benefits should be one of the major factors to consider on whether to proceed with the initiative. The net result of realized benefits less the cost of achieving these benefits (i.e., its value) should be sufficient to justify investing in the initiative.

The business case and the benefits realization management plan, which is an input to portfolio management, contains information about the planned benefits, program, and/or project delivery structure, and a suggested approach for measuring and realizing benefits. Benefits categorization, benefits strategic alignment, and benefits valuation are all inputs to decisions regarding the business prioritization of portfolios, programs, and projects.

2.2.3 SPONSORSHIP AND BENEFITS

The successful adoption of benefits realization management starts at the top of an organization, with executive leadership, sponsors, and benefit owners promoting its importance consistently throughout the life cycle of all initiatives.

It is widely recognized that portfolios, programs, and projects are significantly more successful when they have positive leadership and participation from sponsors. Therefore, when sponsors are actively engaged in initiatives, benefits are more likely to be realized.

A sponsor (if not also the benefit owner) can be part of the executive, management, or leadership teams involved with the benefit owners in creating the strategic direction. As part of the effort to achieve results, benefits can be reviewed, added or updated, and evaluated with the sponsor and benefit owners during the following portfolio, program, and project life-cycle activities, such as:

- Steering committee meetings;
- Stakeholder reviews;
- Portfolio, program, and project progress reviews and status reports; and
- Benefits realization analysis in addition to or in conjunction with lessons learned.

2.3 BRM CORE PRINCIPLES

There are five core principles (Sections 2.3.1 through 2.3.5) that should be considered as guidance for BRM within the context of the three domains of portfolio, program, and project management. These same principles also guide the other parts of an organization when addressing BRM.

These principles carry no specific weighting or order and, to a greater or lesser degree, they each need to be appropriately considered for conducting BRM.

These principles are intended to guide the behavior and thinking of the highest-level executives, benefit owners, senior organizational leaders, other stakeholders, and beneficiaries of planned benefits, as well as portfolio, program, and project managers and their teams engaged in BRM.

2.3.1 NET BENEFITS JUSTIFY THE USE OF INVESTED RESOURCES

Outcomes deliver benefits against funded investments made in pursuit of the organization's strategic goals and business objectives, for which management of the portfolio, program, or project is undertaken.

The rationale for this principle is that the net planned benefits are what justifies the sponsoring organization to use valuable resources on the effort. Value needs to take into account the benefits and the investment in the resources required to realize benefits.

2.3.2 COMMENCEMENT OF WORK IS DRIVEN BY BENEFITS IDENTIFICATION

Planned benefits during development and after delivery of outputs require clear identification *before* the work commences. These benefits should be unambiguously articulated to all delivery stakeholders and beneficiaries.

The rationale for this principle is that delivering the expected value from planned benefits is what guides the thinking and decision making about the work to be undertaken. The value derived from benefits management should be clearly articulated so that all decision makers are able to make informed decisions regarding the work to be undertaken to eventually realize planned benefits.

2.3.3 PLANNED BENEFITS ARE IDENTIFIED IN AUTHORIZING DOCUMENTS

All planned benefits should be appraised, estimated, verified, and agreed by the organization, key stakeholders, and appropriate beneficiaries in an authorizing document (business case, benefits management realization plan, and portfolio/program/project charter). These benefits are monitored and managed as part of the portfolio, program, and project management life cycles.

The rationale for this principle is to effectively appraise, formally document, monitor, and measure planned outcomes and benefits. This enables the organization to effectively monitor progress toward achieving those planned benefits.

2.3.4 BENEFITS REALIZATION IS HOLISTICALLY PLANNED AND MANAGED

Benefits realization is considered holistically, planned and managed from the organization's perspective of needs and requirements, and not limited to those of the portfolio, program, or project delivery.

The rationale for this principle is that BRM extends beyond the portfolio, program, and project domains to the entire enterprise. For BRM to be successful, a broader, holistic perspective of the sponsoring organization should be built into the overall planning approach. This reduces the likelihood of shortcomings that may stem from the narrower focus of delivering only outputs through portfolio, program, and project management efforts. A holistic approach also includes taking unexpected changes into account, with opportunities and threats for benefits realization aligned to organizational goals.

2.3.5 GOVERNANCE AND ADEQUATE RESOURCES ARE ESSENTIAL TO BRM SUCCESS

BRM requires adequately provisioned resources, working within a clear governance structure, with those responsible for managing and achieving the agreed outcomes being identified correctly as accountable and authorized to do so.

The rationale for this principle is that organizations should invest resources and effort to realize and sustain benefits. In addition, organizations should invest in the appropriate level of resources. Organizations should provide a clear and adequate governance structure. They should give authority to the appropriate individuals and hold them accountable for overall success.

2.4 BRM CRITICAL SUCCESS ENABLERS

Critical success enablers (CSEs) for BRM are capabilities that contribute to the effectiveness and efficiency of an organization's efforts. These enablers help improve BRM performance by encouraging organizational leaders to clearly articulate planned benefits while thoroughly thinking through and preparing for outcomes anticipated as leading to realization and sustainment of those benefits. Shortcomings in establishing these enablers can lead to poor performance in realizing the benefits being pursued by the organization.

Specifically, an organization's portfolio, program, and project initiatives may have been viewed as successful (on time, on budget, and to scope), but planned benefits may not have been realized. If this is the case, the organization's strategy and objectives would not have been met. In this context, the outputs would be considered a failure even though the initiatives performed as required. This results in the program or project manager being successful as planned, but being considered responsible for not achieving the value of the planned benefits the customer/owner/sponsor was expecting. The reasons for this type and other failures are many, but one of the leading causes is the organization's failure to provide the critical enablers to help deliver success. Thus, the need to accurately define CSEs is an essential contributor to successful management of benefits realization.

Employing CSEs in portfolio, program, and project initiatives directly improves the organization's ability to achieve intended outcomes and planned benefits. Having CSEs in place helps an organization effectively manage each initiative's trajectory and performance. The definitions and use of these critical success enablers are outlined in Sections 2.4.1 through 2.4.6.

2.4.1 ESTABLISH CLEAR BRM ROLES AND RESPONSIBILITIES

A key to successful BRM is the need for assigned benefit owners or sponsors and other involved leaders to be aligned with the organization's governance structure and BRM strategy. These roles have the accountability and responsibility to lead across the BRM life cycle, which is the management of a benefit from conception through realization and sustainment, expressed in the generic stages of Identify, Execute, and Sustain. Other senior leaders may be responsible to help manage change associated with reaching and realizing planned benefits, which are vital for ensuring overall portfolio, program, and project success. The use of RACI charts or similar techniques is a key way of clearly identifying accountabilities and responsibilities for key roles. These roles need visibility and insight into the programs and projects, and how strategic alignment, objectives, and related benefits are delivered. Benefit owners with the right insight provide the broad-view perspective and guide the overall portfolios, programs, and projects to better address the strategic intent of the planned benefits.

BRM helps to create visibility and insight regarding strategy, and it highlights deviations between program/project outputs and planned outcomes. This insight provides benefit owners the opportunity to make corrections, where small changes can make a big difference. BRM also ensures executives can make decisions to support those programs and projects that directly link to the strategy. Benefit owners, sponsors, and other senior leaders can support BRM by reinforcing accountabilities throughout the associated portfolios, programs, and projects and by serving as role-models for positive BRM behaviors.

2.4.2 DEVELOP THE RIGHT BRM CULTURE

Every organization profits by encouraging and reinforcing the adoption of BRM concepts, terminology, and processes across the portfolios, programs, and projects they commission. This enables the organization to build a BRM culture where executives, initiative leaders, suppliers, individual contributors, and stakeholders are able to easily identify and observe the intended outcomes, results, and benefits that are critical to each initiative's success.

The attributes of a BRM culture may include:

◆ Incorporating benefits formally in every business case, benefits realization management plan, and other initiating tools such as charters;

◆ Assessing portfolios, programs, and projects to ensure they align with strategic organizational objectives, targets, and planned benefits;

◆ Focusing on both tangible and intangible benefits, in addition to any related foreseen risks and their relationship to success;

◆ Establishing appropriate levels of governance with active engagement and shared responsibility among senior executives, those who identify targeted benefits for the sponsored programs and projects, and the managers who lead the delivery of realizing those planned benefits;

◆ Ensuring decision making related to benefits realization is characterized by effective, holistic problem solving;

◆ Encouraging initiative leaders to raise and prioritize issues that affect benefits realization early; and

◆ Demonstrating an awareness, through behaviors and words, of how the organizational culture can positively or negatively impact planned benefits.

Conversely, there are some organizational attributes that can prevent the successful engagement of BRM within an organization. These should be avoided and discouraged, including:

◆ Punishing leaders and team members who share real initiative problems and issues;

◆ Focusing on staying on schedule regardless of impact to cost, quality, benefits, outcome, or result; and

◆ Ambiguous or poor communications that withhold important information.

To achieve success, leaders should encourage behaviors that create the organizational culture inspiring and improving performance across the organization. BRM is a critical enabler to this success, for the senior executives; business owners; and portfolio, program, and project leaders.

2.4.3 BUILD THE RIGHT SKILL SETS

Developing skills to support BRM leads to a greater likelihood for success and improved achievement of planned benefits. BRM involves a variety of roles (see Section 2.2) with levels of engagement that can be clustered into four groups of skill sets:

◆ **Governance roles.** Governance roles include executives, senior management, leadership, and sponsors. Decision-making capabilities, leadership skills, and business acumen are needed to perform the governance roles associated with BRM. In addition to these generalized senior management skills, additional, more specific skills are necessary to enable senior leaders to:

- Design and validate the governance roles, responsibilities, and governance body configuration;
- Establish benefits management criteria, metrics to be monitored, and measurement parameters;
- Review and approve benefits realization management plans;
- Evaluate and approve chartering documents;
- Assess performance against benefits realization criteria and measures at planned intervals;
- Monitor, report, and publish progress against benefit targets for review by all levels of the organization; and
- Identify and make changes to portfolio components (e.g., programs, projects, and operations) to achieve and sustain planned benefits.

Additional guidance on establishing effective governance for portfolios, programs, and projects can be found in *Governance of Portfolios, Programs, and Projects: A Practice Guide* [5]. Further guidance on developing portfolio, program, and project manager competence can be found in *Project Manager Competency Development Framework* – Third Edition [6].

◆ **Stakeholder roles.** Stakeholder roles include middle management, operational management, and/or benefit owners, sponsors, and beneficiaries. These roles are performed by either (a) clients of the benefits being sought or (b) suppliers of resources and capabilities needed to create the outputs and outcomes necessary for realization of the benefits. These stakeholders have a very active role in the Identify stage of the BRM life cycle and should be able to:

- Identify initiatives that can lead to the realization of the strategic benefits from a bottom up perspective;
- Understand the value-for-money considerations in order to validate benefit profiles;
- Aid in the development, appraisal, and approval of value/benefit maps;
- Validate benefit measurement baselines and targets; and
- Give input to transition plans and lessons learned reviews as lessons are learned and periodically reviewed throughout the initiative.

◆ **Managerial roles.** Managerial roles include benefits, portfolio, program, project, and change managers. These roles are responsible for managing the contribution of their area of expertise to the overall benefits throughout the BRM life cycle. These roles report to governance roles and interact with stakeholders and specialist roles.

Organizational project management capabilities as defined in *Project Manager's Competency Development Framework (PMCDF)* [6] apply to these roles.

According to *Managing Change in Organizations: A Practice Guide* [7], successful change management provides organizations with a competitive advantage. A few critical success factors for successful change management (also referred to as organizational change management (OCM)) are: effective communication, addressing potential resistance, team collaboration, and the active support of the sponsor.

- **Specialist roles.** Specialist roles include benefits/business analysis. The skill set of benefits/business analysis comprises (a) analyzing and interpreting complex organizational data; (b) identifying problems and opportunities; (c) providing possible solutions that would yield benefits; and (d) developing dashboards, reports, and presentations. In addition to these skill sets, the roles need excellent communication skills with the ability to interact with and influence a wide range of leadership roles; senior stakeholders; and portfolio, program, project, and change managers. More specifically those engaged in benefit/business analysis should be able to:

  - Facilitate workshops with governance, stakeholders, and managers to identify and select benefits and to develop specific measures and mechanisms for measuring benefits;
  - Create a benefits traceability matrix or a benefits map showing the relationships between planned benefits and their enabling outcomes, capabilities, and initiatives;
  - Review portfolio, program, and project charters against these initiative outputs and outcomes in their business case and benefits realization management plan to confirm their continuing alignment with business needs and expectations;
  - Assess at regular intervals whether the benefits defined in the business case, benefits realization management plan, and initiative charter as captured in the benefits map are being realized by the operations/beneficiaries; and
  - Support portfolio, program, project, and change managers to ensure that all plans, outputs, and outcomes are aligned to the planned benefits.

  A list of additional important skills and expertise is provided in *The PMI Guide to Business Analysis* [8].

2.4.4 EMBRACE FLEXIBILITY

Organizations that tend to be good at BRM embrace flexibility, because in dynamic and changing environments, few programs or projects are delivered as originally planned. This implies that either BRM may not deliver the planned benefits, or that expectations change during the delivery timeline. As the delivery environment changes, the benefits being sought may also need to be changed/adapted.

For example, when managing the benefits of an asset-value project/initiative, such as a construction project, the planned timeline is generally long and subject to the unexpected changes in external environmental economics, which are out of the control of those involved in the physical delivery. The original list of planned benefits captured in the benefits register or map may change; therefore, the list needs to change and be adapted to the new situation.

2.4.5 STRENGTHEN GOVERNANCE AND RISK MANAGEMENT

All portfolios of programs and projects pose a degree of risk. Risks can range from discrete risks that only affect a given program or project to overall risks that can affect the portfolio and the organization itself. Efforts undertaken by an organization to deliver the benefits being sought can also bring disbenefits to the organization or other beneficiaries. (See Section 3.5.3 for a discussion on disbenefits.) Identification of key risks and appropriate governance structures are essential to ensure that the delivery of programs and projects remains credible, appropriate, and useful in achieving planned benefits for the beneficiaries. Once a program or project is closed and the associated risk register is updated, any residual risks are moved to the next higher level in the governance structure for further monitoring or follow-up.

BRM can be embedded into existing governance structures for portfolios, programs, and projects where they may already exist. When BRM is not already embedded in these governance structures, steps should be taken to ensure BRM is part of the governance of portfolios, programs, and projects. This is key to ensuring benefits and value are being pursued and remain aligned with the organization's overall strategy. BRM provides the necessary monitoring and management mechanisms to track whether the benefits are actually realized. The governance structures also need to provide a way of ensuring benefits are sustained after program and project completion. These structures should also ensure adequate BRM metrics are available to monitor both tangible and intangible benefits, which are viewed as an integral part of ongoing portfolio, program, and project governance.

2.4.6 ESTABLISH BENEFITS TRACKING

Benefits tracking involves identifying appropriate BRM metrics for use in effective management and leadership. This is essential to achieve the outputs and outcomes of the portfolios, programs, and projects in addition to the benefits for the beneficiaries. BRM metrics need to address both tangible and intangible benefits, as applicable. This allows the tracking of progress toward benefits realization. BRM metrics are not required to be precise or holistic, but they should be viewed as essential to providing insight into trends and allowing a degree of forecasting for successful realization. Such forecasting is indicative of outcomes, and when necessary, can help improve portfolio, program, and project initiatives to help ensure benefits realization.

Appropriate, measurable, and an understood set of BRM metrics should be in place early to enable adequate monitoring. The measurement of benefits and their associated value, as it materializes before, during, and after realization, is critical to successful BRM.

2.5 ORGANIZATIONAL BRM ROLES AND RESPONSIBILITIES

BRM roles and responsibilities include many of those associated with portfolio, program, and project management, and include organizational roles focused specifically on benefits management activities. These roles and responsibilities are applied throughout the BRM life cycle. An individual may also have operational or portfolio, program, and project roles that include BRM responsibilities. For example, senior managers may have benefits realization management responsibilities for programs and projects that originate in their department. Portfolio managers may have responsibilities for benefits realization for portfolios. Business analysts may have responsibilities for benefits tracking and measurement. Depending on the size and type of organization or business environment, an individual may fulfill multiple benefits management roles and responsibilities. The use of responsibility assignment matrices (RAM) or RACI charts are helpful techniques for ensuring the clarity of benefits-related roles and responsibilities. Figure 2-4 offers a general overview of how these roles may be seen in an organization.

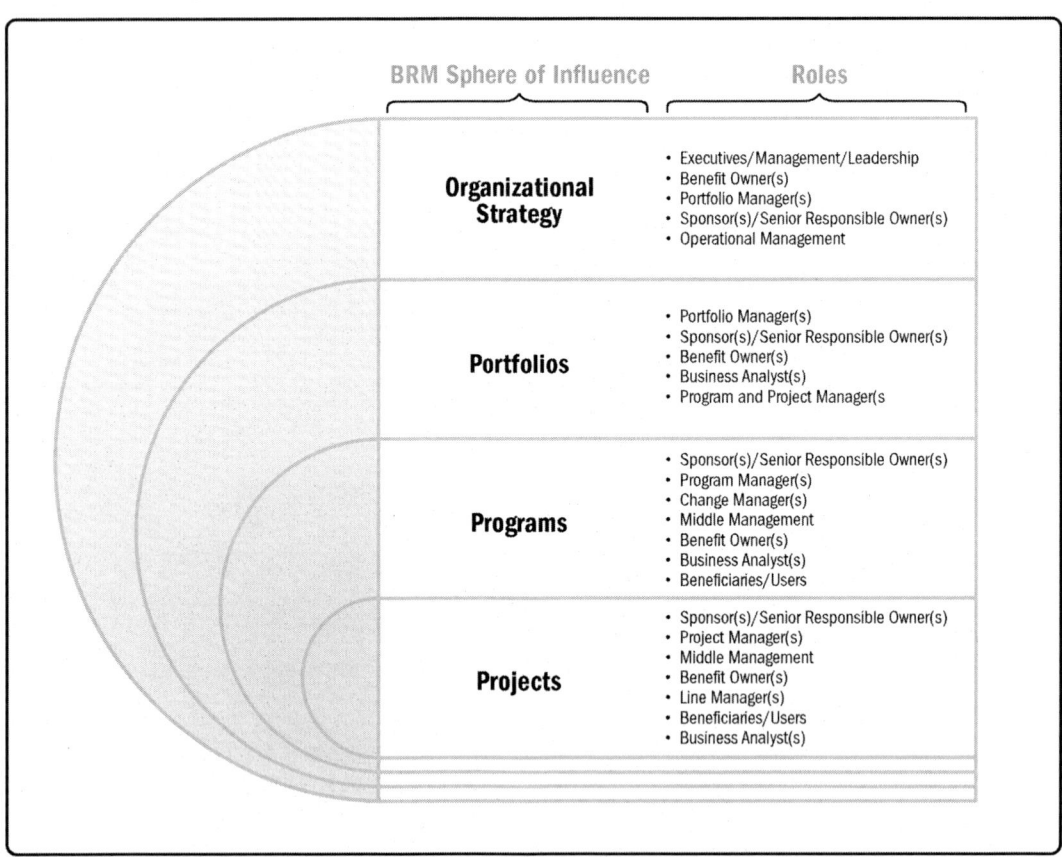

Figure 2-4. BRM Sphere of Influence and Roles

2.5.1 ORGANIZATIONAL STRATEGY AND SPONSORSHIP

Benefits are determined at the outset of a portfolio, program, or project through the creation, definition, and execution of an organizational benefits realization management strategy. BRM strategy is the organization's high-level direction for managing planned benefits achieved through portfolio, program, and project outputs and resulting outcomes. This is set by the leadership team, for example, executives and management of any organization (not-for-profit, private, public, government, etc.). For organizations that implement program management offices (PMO) or enterprise program management offices (EPMO), these often play a key role in helping to determine benefits realization strategies for the organization. Table 2-1 identifies BRM roles and responsibilities at the organizational strategy level.

Table 2-1. Typical Organizational Strategic Roles and Responsibilities in BRM

Role	Description and Responsibilities
Executives/Management/Leadership	• Description: The individual or group accountable for the organization's strategic goals and objectives. • Defines strategic goals, objectives, and benefits for each initiative • Establishes, communicates, and actively supports the organizational strategy as well as the benefits of the strategy • Approves organization's BRM policy and practices • Identifies initiatives that support attaining strategic goals and objectives • Meets with senior management/leadership teams to review status of initiatives undertaken to execute strategy and realize benefits
Benefit Owner(s)	• Description: The individual or group accountable for benefits realization. • Works closely with executives/management/leadership to identify, track, and document benefits aligned with the strategic goals and objectives of the sponsoring organization • Ensures measurement methods for planned benefits are in place and evaluation occurs from start to finish of the delivery process • Ensures planned benefits are realized and sustained per benefits realization management plan • May also serve the role of sponsor or operational manager
Portfolio Manager(s)	• Description: The individual or group assigned to the performing organization to establish, balance, monitor, and control portfolio components in order to achieve strategic business objectives. • Manages portfolio components to achieve strategic business objectives and related benefits aligned with the portfolio they manage • Liaises with executives/management/leadership team to document and break down strategy into business case(s) to support it
Sponsor(s)/Senior Responsible Owner(s)	• Description: The individual or group that provides resources and support for the portfolio, program, or project and is accountable for enabling success. • Ensures portfolios, programs, and projects meet their objectives that lead to planned benefits • Provides resources and support for the portfolios, programs, and projects undertaken by the organization to help enable successful realization of the benefits • Ensures engagement with middle management, benefit owner(s), and beneficiaries to support results • Ensures engagement with middle management, benefit owner(s), and beneficiaries to drive responsibility and accountability • May also serve the role of benefit owner
Middle (Functional) Management	• Description: The group responsible for the day-to-day operational activities of the organization and for incorporating the activities to sustain and promote realized benefits into business as usual. • Works closely with executives, other organizational management and leadership, and portfolio managers to identify and implement benefits-sustaining activities for incorporating realized benefits into the day-to-day operations, as well as outside the organization, as appropriate • May also serve the role of benefit owner

2.5.2 PORTFOLIO ROLES AND BRM

A portfolio is a collection of projects, programs, subsidiary portfolios, and operations managed as a group to achieve strategic objectives [9]. In a portfolio, planned benefits tend to be stated at a high level, addressing more than one business objective, and apply to an entire portfolio of programs and projects. These benefits are attained through the portfolio, program, and project outputs resulting in the outcomes attained. These outcomes lead to the benefits realized by the organization and, ultimately, the value pursued by the organization. The high level of benefits tied to portfolios can encompass more supporting benefits needed to achieve any given higher-level benefit. For example, increased customer satisfaction takes into account benefits that are normally applied at the program level, such as ease of reporting outages and reduced manual effort. However, the levels of value that the organization seeks may take the outcomes and realized benefits of several components of the portfolio.

The portfolio management structure is a natural fit for BRM. Plans need to include and incorporate common, complementary, and supporting policies and practices.

The roles associated with deriving and achieving benefits from a portfolio perspective are listed in Table 2-2. These are guidelines—roles and responsibilities may be combined to suit the organization's need.

Table 2-2. Typical Portfolio Roles and Responsibilities in BRM

Role	Description and Responsibilities
Portfolio Manager(s)	• Description: The individual or group assigned to the performing organization to establish, balance, monitor, and control portfolio components in order to achieve strategic business objectives. • Oversees portfolio and ensures benefits realization • Collaborates with benefit owners to establish benefit measures for planned benefits within the portfolios they manage • Creates business case to justify initiatives, outline benefits and value
Sponsor(s)/Senior Responsible Owner(s)	• Description: The individual or a group that provides resources and support for the portfolio, program, or project and is accountable for enabling success. • Provides clear direction for the portfolio and realization of planned benefits • Ensures engagement with middle management, benefit owner(s), and beneficiaries to support results • Ensures engagement with middle management, benefit owner(s), and beneficiaries to drive responsibility and accountability • May also serve the role of benefit owner
Benefit Owner(s)	• Description: The individual or group accountable for benefits realization. • Works closely with portfolio manager to ensure planned benefits are managed • Ensures measurement methods for planned benefits are in place and evaluation occurs from start to finish of the delivery process • Manages benefits realization management plan • May also serve the role of sponsor
Business Analyst(s)	• Description: The individual or group that works to perform activities to support delivery of solutions that align to business objectives and provide continuous value to the organization. • Works with portfolio managers to lead the programs and projects chartered for creating the outcomes that lead to the benefits being sought in order to achieve the organization's strategic goals
Program and Project Managers	• Description: See descriptions under program ad project roles and responsibilities. • Works with portfolio managers to lead the programs and projects chartered for creating the outputs resulting in outcomes that lead to the benefits being sought to achieve the organization's strategic goals and objectives

2.5.3 PROGRAM ROLES AND BRM

A program is defined as related projects, subsidiary programs, and program activities managed in a coordinated manner to obtain benefits not available from managing them individually [10]. While organizational strategy and, to some extent, portfolio strategy are created to guide the organization, programs and projects are a means to produce outputs that yield outcomes that are leveraged to realize benefits.

A program should keep the benefits realization management plan and the benefits register up to date, so that any changes during the course of constituent projects delivery are reflected in the plan and the register, which is a repository in which benefit profiles are recorded. Any risk to the program that might prevent planned benefits from being achieved should be added to the risk management registers and plans.

The roles and responsibilities associated with BRM at the program level are listed in Table 2-3.

Table 2-3. Typical Program Roles and Responsibilities in BRM

Role	Description and Responsibilities
Sponsor(s)/ Senior Responsible Owner(s)	• Description: The individual or group that provides resources and support for the portfolio, program, or project and is accountable for enabling success. • Commissions the program • Ensures projects or programs meet their objectives supporting planned benefits • Provides clear direction for the program and its planned benefits • Ensures engagement with middle and upper management, benefit owner(s), and beneficiaries to support results • May also serve as benefit owner
Program Manager(s)	• Description: The individual or group authorized by the performing organization to lead the teams responsible for achieving program objectives. • Ensures that the overall program structure and applied program management processes enable the program and its component teams to successfully complete the work or outputs that support the realization of planned benefits • Integrates the program components' outputs into the program's end product, services, or results, such that beneficiaries realize planned benefits • Collaborates with benefit owners to establish benefit measures for planned benefits within the programs they manage
Change Manager(s)	• Description: The individual or group tasked with ensuring the change is introduced to the organization in a structured and planned manner. • Explains benefits of change initiatives to all stakeholders and applies organizational change management techniques to ensure comprehension • Provides insight to the program manager about potential impacts, both positive or negative, that could affect benefits realization
Middle (Functional) Management	• Description: The group responsible for the day-to-day operational activities of the organization and for incorporating the activities to sustain and promote realized benefits into business as usual • Works with program and change management to disseminate benefit information to operational teams • Escalates benefits-related risks to the program manager and sponsor • Oversees changes and participates in output ownership transfer
Benefit Owner(s)	• Description: The individual or group accountable for benefits realization. • Works closely with program manager to ensure planned benefits are managed, as well as identify any new benefits or disbenefits throughout program duration • Ensures measurement methods for planned benefits are in place and evaluation occurs from start to finish of the delivery process • Manages benefits realization management plan (often after program completion) • May also serve as sponsor or operational manager
Business Analyst(s)	• Description: The individual or group that works to perform activities to support delivery of solutions that align to business objectives and provide continuous value to the organization. • Works with the program manager to perform business case validation, scenario planning, ascertain currency of the benefits realization management plan, support the program management plan(s), and help ensure realization of benefits
Beneficiaries/Users	• Description: The designated individual or organization that receives gains from planned and realized benefits. • Liaise with sponsor(s), benefit owner(s), program managers, project teams, and others where applicable to help optimize benefits realization

2.5.4 PROJECT ROLES AND BRM

A project is a temporary endeavor undertaken to create a unique product, service, or result [2]. Benefits are generally realized through usage and outcomes of those products, services, or results.

The roles and responsibilities associated with BRM at the project level are shown in Table 2-4.

Table 2-4. Typical Project Roles and Responsibilities in BRM

Role	Description and Responsibilities
Sponsor(s)/Senior Responsible Owner(s)	• Description: The individual or a group that provides resources and support for the portfolio, program, or project and is accountable for enabling success. • Commissions the project • Ensures projects or programs meet their objectives and deliver planned benefits • Provides clear direction for the project on how its outputs contribute to planned benefits • Ensures engagement with middle and upper management, benefit owner(s), and beneficiaries to support results • May also serve as benefit owner
Project Manager(s)	• Description: The individual or group assigned by the performing organization to lead the teams that are responsible for achieving the project objectives. • Oversees project and ensures output delivery to support the realization of planned benefits • Collaborates with benefit owners to establish benefit measures for planned benefits within the programs they manage
Middle (Functional) Management	• Description: The group responsible for the day-to-day operational activities of the organization and for incorporating the activities to sustain and promote realized benefits into business as usual. • Works with project manager to disseminate benefit information to operational teams • Effects benefit risk escalation to project manager(s) and/or sponsor(s) • Oversees changes and participates in output ownership transfer
Benefit Owner(s)	• Description: The individual or group accountable for benefits realization. • Works with project manager to ensure planned benefits are managed, as well as identify any new benefits or disbenefits throughout project duration • Manages the benefits realization management plan • Ensures measurement methods for planned benefits are in place and evaluation occurs from start to finish of the delivery process • Responsible for benefits realization (often after project completion) • May also serve as sponsor or operational manager
Beneficiaries/Users	• Description: The designated individual or organization that receives gains from planned benefits and their realization. • Liaises with sponsor(s), benefit owner(s), project teams, and others where applicable to help optimize benefit realization
Business Analyst(s)	• Description: The individual or group that works to perform activities to support delivery of solutions that align to business objectives and provide continuous value to the organization. • Elicits and manages requirements to achieve project deliverables, including measurement and realization of benefits • Assists the transitioning of ownership outputs to beneficiaries and facilitates planned outcomes and benefits as appropriate

3

BRM FRAMEWORK

The BRM framework is an integrated set of governance and management practices designed to define, develop, deliver, and sustain planned benefits derived from the outputs of portfolios, programs, and projects. It includes a life cycle structure, key activities with associated roles and responsibilities, and depicts their general relationships. The BRM life cycle component of the framework is expressed in the stages of Identify, Execute, and Sustain.

Using a framework helps organizations to focus on the reasons for undertaking projects and programs—the realization of benefits created through their outputs. This framework is intended as guidance for practitioners and can be adapted for use in their organizations.

The assumptions underpinning this generic BRM framework include:

- ◆ The organization owns the BRM framework, which reflects its BRM strategy consistently with its overall approach to strategic planning, goal setting, and related initiatives.
- ◆ The BRM framework echoes the organization's value-oriented mindset.
- ◆ The BRM framework supports and guides development of a benefit from concept to realization and into sustainment.
- ◆ Benefits may be realized by operations and other internal/external beneficiaries and stakeholders.
- ◆ Benefit owners have the authority, responsibility, and accountability for benefits realization.
- ◆ Portfolio, program, and project managers have specific and clearly delimited roles and responsibilities across the BRM life cycle.
- ◆ The BRM framework supports the delivery of each type of benefit to be created by outputs of portfolios, programs, and projects. It should also allow for the fact that the realization of multiple benefits can be underway at any given time.
- ◆ Activities associated within the life-cycle stage of the BRM framework may or may not be sequential processes.

- The BRM framework and its life cycle are scalable and can be adapted to an organization's existing benefits management related activities, including portfolio, program, and project management life cycles.
- Once realized, the benefits are sustained (or adapted) with the right monitoring by the benefit owners and appropriate beneficiaries and other stakeholders.
- The efficacy of the BRM framework depends upon timely, transparent communications and a commitment to continuous improvement through lessons learned.

Figure 3-1 serves as an organizing model for practitioners to use as is or to tailor BRM for organization-specific applications.

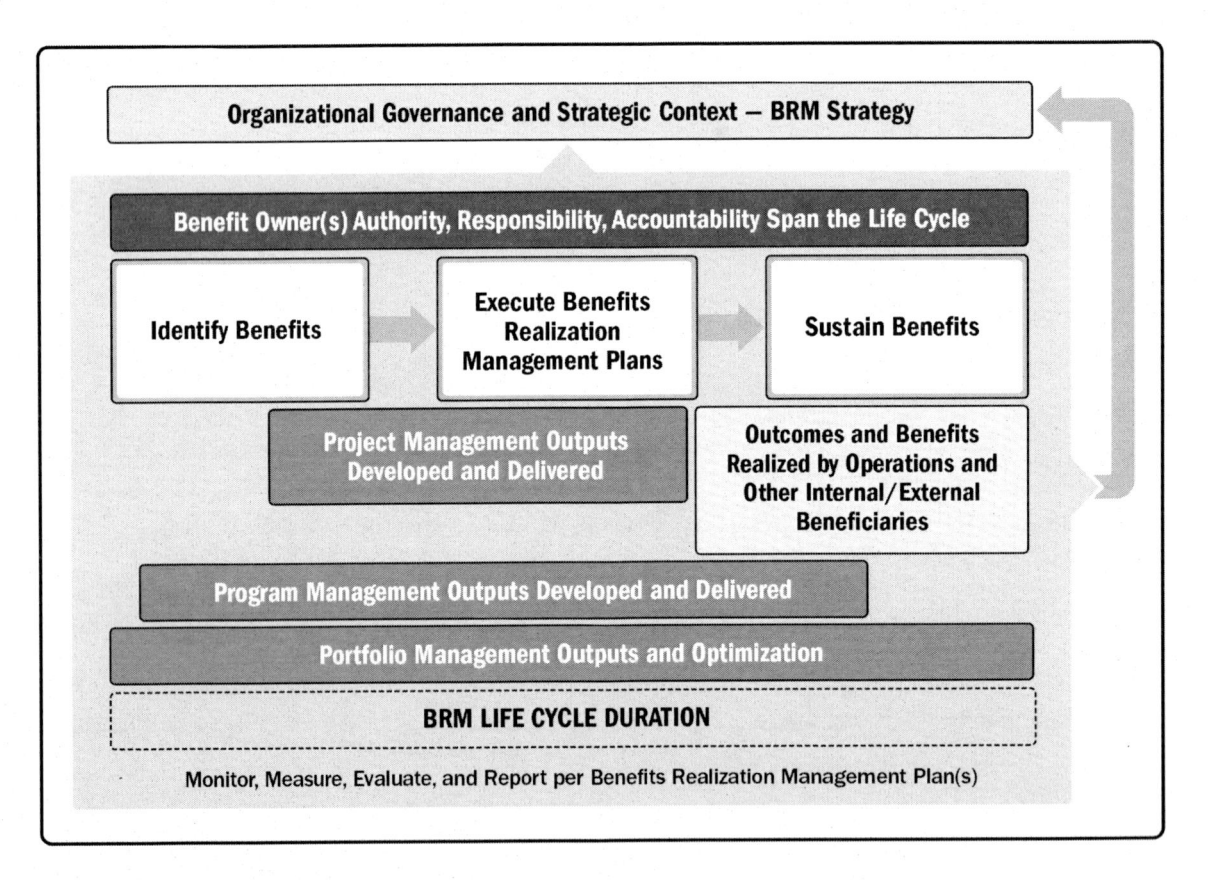

Figure 3-1. BRM Framework in the Context of Portfolios, Programs, and Projects

3.1 OVERVIEW

The *PMI Thought Leadership Series—Benefits Realization Management Framework* [11] defined three major periods, now known as stages, of a BRM life cycle: Identify, Execute, and Sustain.

- ◆ **Identify.** The organization's leadership defines the benefits it intends to create through the outputs of portfolios of programs and projects.
- ◆ **Execute.** The work of portfolios, programs, and projects is performed in this stage to create the outputs (planned deliverables) that lead to the intended outcomes and benefits realization.
- ◆ **Sustain.** The benefit owner and beneficiary (who may be the same person or organization), realize the planned benefit. This stage is also where a benefit may be adapted in certain circumstances.

The BRM framework is not intended to generate another separate management function; organizations integrate it within its existing governance and general management structure.

The executive leadership team should fully define and approve what types of programs and projects fall within the BRM framework and decide who or what group has authority and responsibility for the overall viability of the framework and its life cycle. This is essential to the organization's BRM strategy.

Sections 3.2 through 3.4 further describe the life-cycle stages of the framework.

3.2 IDENTIFY STAGE

In this stage, the organization's executive leadership decides what benefits to pursue and whether portfolios, programs, and projects are the best route to achieve strategic objectives and their associated benefits. Planned benefits are then defined and organized. Each benefit should have a designated owner.

Ideas for benefits come from many sources. Commonly, strategic planning workshops, annual budgeting planning, updates of benefits mapping, and stakeholder insight identify potential benefits followed by their qualification and quantification. Quantification includes forecasting or estimating the scale of benefits anticipated to be achieved through a portfolio of programs and projects.

3.2.1 DEVELOP BUSINESS CASE AND BENEFITS REALIZATION MANAGEMENT PLAN

Within the organization's governance, management structure, and delegated authorities, a designated individual or group of individuals evaluate and propose potential work together with associated benefits consistent with BRM strategy.

Whatever way an organization uses to conceive and evaluate opportunities, goals, and associated benefits to be achieved, it should also include a benefits realization plan for each benefit. This plan is separate but consistent with the business case. Between the two, the following questions concerning benefits are addressed:

◆ Do benefits align with the organization's strategic goals and their associated objectives?
◆ Are they tangible or intangible benefits, or are they short- or long-term benefits as explicitly defined in the business case?
◆ Have associated risks, including potential disbenefits, been identified for managing?
◆ Does the business case outline how benefits should be measured and when they are forecasted for delivery?
◆ Does the measurement of the benefits necessitate new outputs or activities that should be included in the business case?
◆ Are all project or program benefits adequately documented?
◆ Have key stakeholders signed off on each benefits realization plan?
◆ How does governance factor into the benefits realization plan, including relevant acceptance criteria?
◆ Are project selection and/or funding decisions based on the impact of planned benefits?
◆ Have the owners and beneficiaries been consulted and confirmed?

3.2.2 AUTHORIZE CHARTER

Each organization should have its own criteria for a business case and benefits realization management plan. The general concept for the benefits realization management plan is shown in Figure 3-2.

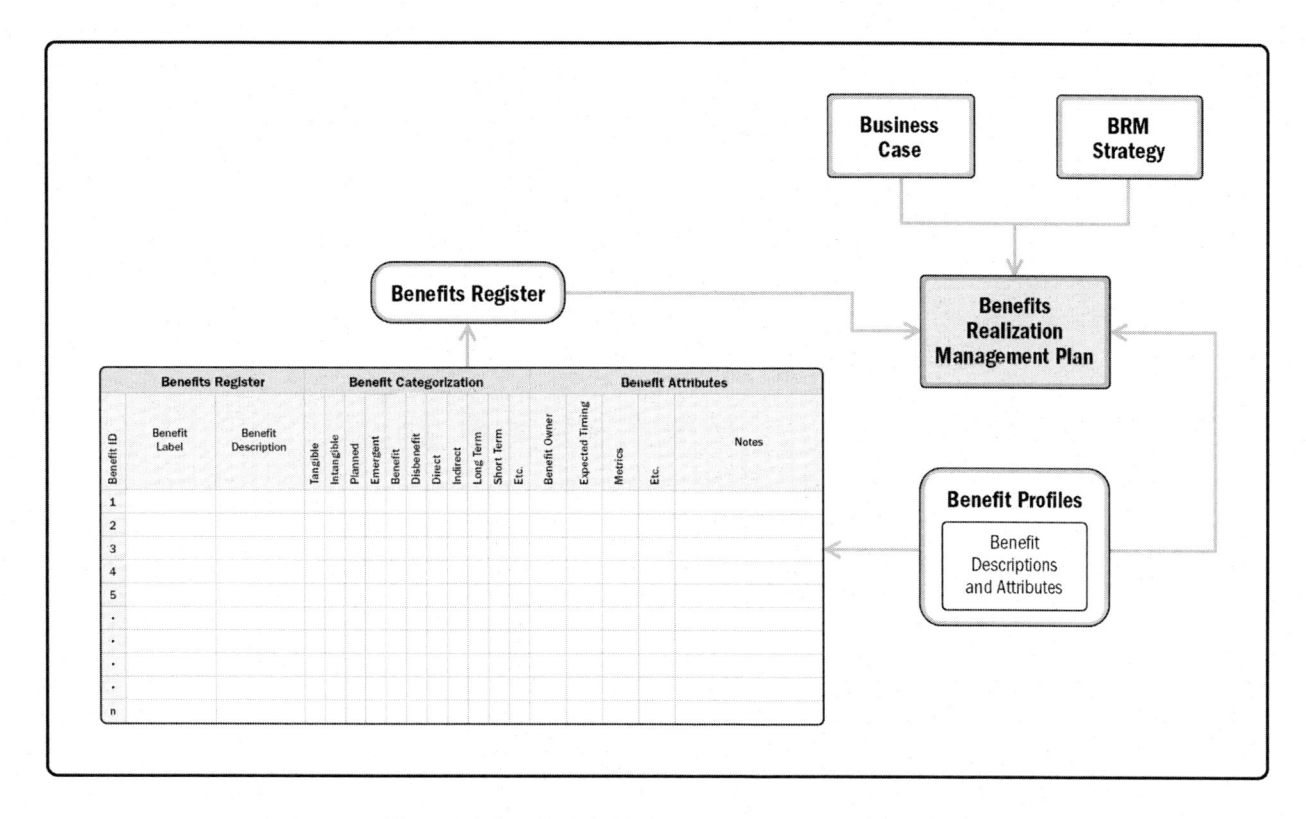

Figure 3-2. Benefits Realization Management Plan Concept

For additional information about the elements of the benefits realization management plan, refer to Section 3.5.2.

The business case and the benefits realization plan are authorized, then a charter initiates the appropriate portfolio, program, and project work. It is at this point that the assigned benefit owner takes full leadership responsibility and accountability across the entire BRM life cycle for the realization of each benefit.

3.3 EXECUTE STAGE

During this stage, portfolios, programs and/or projects begin technical and management planning to create the outputs—products, services, and capabilities—that will lead to outcomes for beneficiaries to realize planned benefits.

The benefit owner is responsible to ensure that:

- Planned benefits are clearly communicated to key stakeholders.
- Program or project teams understand how their outputs contribute to planned benefits.
- Progress reviews are punctual.
- There is a clear way of discovering emergent benefits as well as the threat of disbenefits (see Section 3.5.3 for a discussion emergent benefits and disbenefits).
- The program or project remains relevant, aligned, and produces outputs for planned benefits in the face of unexpected events.

3.3.1 DEVELOP OUTPUTS

For each of the programs and projects concerned, this is the stage where the technical work produces outputs that lead to the realization of planned benefits. The benefit owner coordinates with the portfolio, program, and project managers to optimize and eventually realize planned benefits:

- Use phase-gate or similarly designated reviews to ensure programs and projects remain aligned with the organization's strategic objectives.
- Evaluate risks and key performance indicators (KPIs) for stable delivery of benefits.
- Record progress and inform key stakeholders.
- Ensure the planned benefits realization dependencies, components, and management structures are incorporated into the appropriate governance process.
- Ensure key stakeholders and beneficiaries have reviewed, understand, and act in accordance with the planned benefits realization management plan dependencies.
- Understand the impact of benefits to enhance controls and reduce risk.
- Use appropriate communication and stakeholder engagement processes.

3.3.2 DELIVER OUTPUTS AND TRANSFER OWNERSHIP OF OUTPUTS TO REALIZE BENEFITS

The benefit owner needs to work with the appropriate portfolio, program, or project managers to ensure beneficiaries are appropriately engaged and briefed to realize planned benefits. This also includes plans for sustainment of the benefits. For realized benefits to be sustainable within the beneficiary organization, the benefit owner and operational managers responsible for benefit delivery take ownership. This requires incorporating the organizational changes associated with the realized benefits to become part of the organization's business as usual.

3.4 SUSTAIN STAGE

This stage focuses on the acceptance and use of the outputs that create outcomes leading to the realization of benefits. Benefits sustainment, the ongoing activities performed by the benefit owners and beneficiaries, ensures the continuation of outcomes and benefits achieved through portfolio, program, and project outputs. Benefit owners, beneficiaries, and business analysts, rather than program or project managers, typically focus on this stage. Concerns they may need to address, include:

- Are benefits (tangible, intangible, short-term, and/or long-term) being tracked?
- Have outputs been transitioned to and approved by key stakeholders (beneficiaries), including accountable operational or business owners?
- Are realized benefits being measured and verified against applicable plans?
- Are benefits being realized within the timeframe of the benefits realization management plan?
- Have emergent benefits and disbenefits been identified, and if so, are they properly managed?

3.4.1 REALIZE-SUSTAIN BENEFITS

The beneficiaries use portfolio, program, and project outputs to create intended outcomes and then begin to realize benefits. Realization may be immediate or incremental, depending on the type of benefit and its success metrics. When the benefit is realized as planned, monitoring should help to ensure its sustainment, when appropriate. Practices supporting sustainment of benefits include:

- Planning for operational, financial, and behavioral changes, when necessary, by beneficiaries to continue checking benefit performance;
- Performing an audit to verify that the benefits have been realized;
- Facilitating continuous improvement through ongoing knowledge sharing regarding the benefit's contribution to organizational success;

- Developing business cases for (a) the potential initiation of new programs or projects to respond to operational issues or (b) a need for improvement in product performance or functionality; and
- Monitoring the continued suitability of the new capability or other change factors.

3.4.2 ADAPT BENEFITS

Depending upon the type of benefit, whether it is internally or externally realized, it may become necessary to adapt it. Modifying or substituting a benefit may be an option when the full intent of the planned benefit is not met. This can happen when, for example, technological advancement triggers the availability of a new (different) benefit. This can also happen when a benefit becomes a disbenefit due to political or regulatory changes after the original benefit is realized.

3.5 SUPPORTING PRACTICES ACROSS THE BRM LIFE CYCLE

This section identifies important interactions among key participants at each of the life cycle stages. It also describes tools and generally accepted practices for categorizing, measuring, and tracing benefit-related requirements.

3.5.1 KEY INTERACTIONS

Key interactions are:

- **Identify stage.** The benefit owner collaborates with the portfolio or program manager in the development of the business case, benefits realization management plan, and charter. In cases where a project generates the benefit, the project manager should be involved. Business analysts interact with benefit owners consistent with organizational practice.

  The degree of involvement from the portfolio, program, or project managers depends upon the organization's culture and type of programs or projects involved. In some circumstances, an enterprise project management office may be involved. Typically, after approval of the business case and benefits realization management plan, the portfolio manager incorporates the appropriate information into the system.

  The benefit owner, in coordination with key stakeholders, approves, assigns, and starts the monitoring, measuring, evaluating, and reporting of benefit progress throughout the life cycle.

- **Execute stage.** Portfolio and program managers communicate the status and progress toward planned benefits with the benefit owner. The benefit owner keeps the portfolio and program managers apprised of environmental and strategic changes that may affect execution of the benefits realization management plan. Similar activities may arise when a project manager is directly involved, rather than as part of a program.

The benefit owner should ensure that planned monitoring, measuring, evaluating, and reporting of progress occurs. Variances may require adjustments in any of these activities. The benefit owner and/or sponsor's main challenge is optimizing benefits and, when warranted, amending or canceling the benefits realization management plan.

- **Sustain stage.** In this stage, the benefit owner has primary responsibility for overseeing communications with beneficiaries and other stakeholders. This involves continuation of monitoring, measuring, evaluating, and reporting against the original benefits realization management plan. Portfolio managers are more involved than program or project managers. This is dependent upon factors such as the organization's BRM strategy, type of benefit, whether it is internal or external, and strategic shifts in the organization.

Should it become necessary to adapt or substitute a benefit, the benefit owner acts to modify the benefits realization management plan or introduces a new benefit into the Identify stage.

3.5.2 PRINCIPAL SUPPORTING BRM TOOLS

Common tools used in BRM get prepared mainly in the Identify stage. The following summary of tools, which may be used separately, essentially comprise the benefits management plan for each benefit identified and authorized:

- **Benefits quantification.** There are several techniques for benefits quantification, such as evidence-based forecasting or reference class forecasting. The general approach to benefits forecasting consists of (a) evaluating the current (as-is) state of performance set goals for the desired future (to-be) state, (b) developing a procedure to monitor progress toward the target, and (c) defining the owner responsible to monitor and evaluate benefits.

- **Benefits realization management plan.** Generally, each benefit has its own plan that should include topics such as:
  - Contact information for benefit owners and beneficiaries;
  - Mapping of planned benefits to appropriate components;
  - Description of how each benefit should be measured and deemed realized;
  - Key performance indicators and thresholds for evaluating achievement of benefits;
  - Risk assessment and probability for achieving each benefit;

- Status or progress indicators;
- Target dates and milestones for realization;
- Person, group, or organization responsible for delivering each benefit; and
- Tracking and communication processes necessary to record and report status of benefits to stakeholders.

◆ **Benefit profile.** A benefit profile is a description of the benefit, its intended beneficiaries, and criteria for its realization. Completing a profile for each desired benefit helps to analyze the planned benefits. A basic benefit profile describes:

- What the benefit is,
- Benefit's categorization,
- Who the benefit is for,
- When the benefit is intended, and
- Criteria used to measure development and determine its realization.

Such a profile becomes part of the benefits register and supports the benefits realization management plan. More information is added to the profile as development proceeds. Figure 3-3 shows a sample profile.

Benefit Profile

This profile is used to define an understanding of a benefit's attributes and measures:

Initiative Name:		Benefit ID:	
Benefit Name/Label:			
Benefit Description:			
Benefit Categorization (e.g., tangible/intangible, disbenefit, planned/emergent, financial/nonfinancial, etc.)			
Organizational Goal/Objective:			
Benefit Owner:		Key Stakeholders:	
Dependencies:			
Risks:			
Assumptions			
Metrics Description:			
Start Date:	End Date:	Source:	
Responsible Manager:	Reporting Frequency:	Target Value:	

Figure 3-3. Example Benefit Profile

◆ **Benefits register.** This is a repository in which benefit profiles are recorded. The register may be used in aggregated ways at different levels of the organization to fit its needs. For example, a program may have a repository for all its benefits under management. A portfolio may have lists, actual or aggregated, representing multiple programs. Figure 3-4 illustrates a sample benefits register.

Benefits Register			Benefit Categorization										Benefit Attributes				
Benefit ID	Benefit Label	Benefit Description	Tangible	Intangible	Planned	Emergent	Benefit	Disbenefit	Direct	Indirect	Long Term	Short Term	Etc.	Benefit Owner	Expected Timing	Metrics	Etc.	Notes
1																		
2																		
3																		
4																		
5																		
.																		
.																		
.																		
n																		

Figure 3-4. Benefits Register

◆ **Benefits map.** A benefits map is a graphical representation of the relationship of major elements needed to realize a benefit. The benefits map, like the register, can be scaled to the organization, portfolio, program, or project levels of use. It can be for a single benefit or multiple benefits. Benefits maps can include outputs, enablers, change, outcome, benefits, disbenefits, strategic drivers, and objectives. Dependencies are sometimes shown. Figure 3-5 illustrates a typical benefits map.

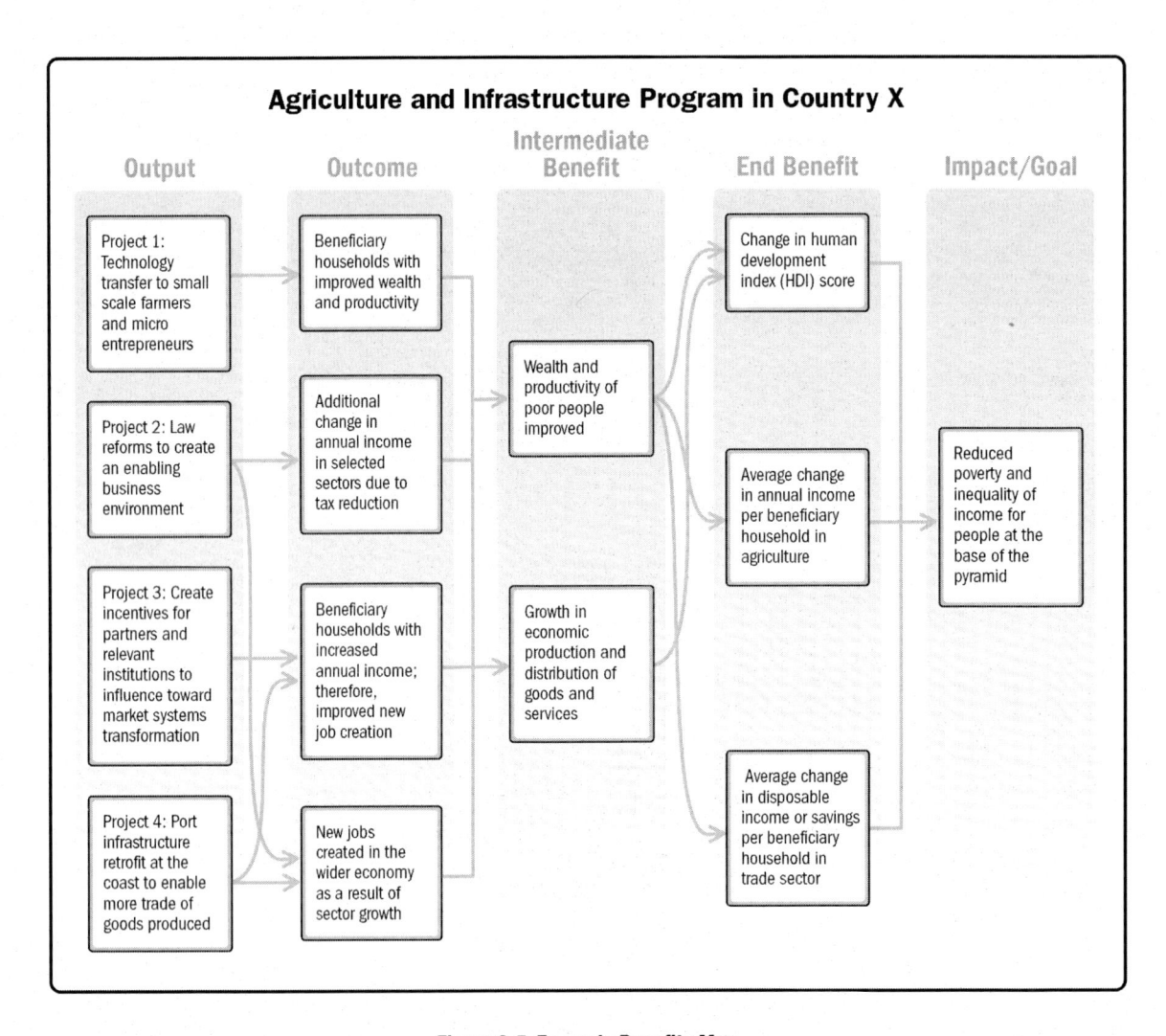

Figure 3-5. Example Benefits Map

- **Benefits traceability matrix.** A benefits traceability matrix is a grid that maps the planned benefits to portfolio, program, and project outputs. The benefits traceability matrix is a component of a benefits realization management plan and may supplement the benefits register. Again, like the benefits register and map, the benefits traceability matrix can be scaled to fit the BRM needs of the organization. Figure 3-6 shows an example of a matrix.

	Deliverables																	
	Portfolio A										Portfolio n							
	Program A			Project B				Project C			Program n			Project n				
Benefits	Deliverable A1	Deliverable A2	Deliverable A3	Deliverable B1	Deliverable B2	Deliverable B3	Deliverable B4	Deliverable C1	Deliverable C2	Deliverable C3	...	...	...	...	...	...	Deliverable n	Notes
Benefit 1																		
Benefit 2																		
Benefit 3																		
•																		
•																		
•																		
•																		
•																		
•																		
Benefit n																		

Figure 3-6. Benefits Traceability Matrix

3.5.3 CATEGORIZING BENEFITS

Organizations face a variety of challenges when pursuing benefits. Categorizing these benefits not only helps to identify and group them, but also guides organizations on how to effectively manage their realization.

One of the main challenges is being able to communicate well with all stakeholders about which benefits are being pursued and why, benefit categories, and how benefits may or may not relate to each other or be realized. One way to improve communication and the understanding of benefits is to develop an approved classification scheme of commonly accepted categories.

Defining and communicating the categories of benefits helps organizations identify appropriate measures for tracking progress toward the attainment and sustainment of benefits. Benefit categories are an important component of the benefit profile of a given benefit and are typically captured in the benefits register.

There is no standard categorization scheme for benefits. Each organization needs to define and agree on the categories of benefits that are important for successful realization.

3.5.3.1 COMMON CATEGORIES OF BENEFITS

The benefit category is a level of benefits classification. The following benefit categories are commonly cited examples.

- **Tangible or intangible benefits:**
  - *Tangible.* Tangible benefits are measured objectively based upon evidence. An example of a tangible benefit is a direct cost reduction. An organization may undertake an improvement effort to reduce the cost associated with providing a given function.
  - *Intangible.* Intangible benefits are those that cannot be directly measured objectively and instead rely on a proxy (or representative) measure or evaluation. Examples of intangible benefits include customer satisfaction, ease of use, and the organization's image or goodwill.
- **Planned or emergent benefits:**
  - *Planned.* Planned benefits are intended gains for a designated beneficiary that is selected and approved through the organization's BRM system. Planned benefits also are known as anticipated benefits or expected benefits. For example, a manufacturer that launches a project to increase the capacity to manufacture its goods would expect a decreased cycle time for filling orders.
  - *Emergent.* Emergent benefits are unexpected benefits that arise during or after a program, project, or within the context of a portfolio. These benefits may have a significant influence on the perceived success of a program or project. If the emergent benefits are positive in nature, they may also positively influence the overall program or project outcomes. Conversely, if the emergent benefits are negative, then the overall view of the project or program may reflect that as well, or possibly be viewed as unsuccessful.

    The identification and assessment of emergent benefits and their overall impact is key to managing benefits realization. Adjustments may be needed to the benefits register or the benefits realization management plan to address any identified emergent benefits. One example of an emergent benefit is improvement in an organization's public image and associated good will toward the organization following the organization's increased involvement in community activities. In this case, the emergent benefit is viewed in a positive light by the community members affected, which then leads to increased sales of the products it produces. Emergent benefits may also be referred to as unplanned or unanticipated benefits.

- ◆ **Direct or indirect benefits:**
    - *Direct.* Direct benefits are unambiguous, measurable gains realized as planned by defined beneficiaries. For example, a customer service provider launches a program to set up additional call centers in multiple time zones to respond to customer calls across these time zones in a more reliable manner. The increased capacity of the call centers are a direct outcome of the expanded call center program with a direct benefit of easier and more timely resolution of customer calls.
    - *Indirect.* Indirect benefits are secondary or incidental gains, planned or unplanned, realized by defined beneficiaries or others upon realization of a direct benefit. For example, the expanded call center program mentioned previously may also deliver an indirect benefit of improved staff satisfaction due to their ability to provide more timely responses to customer requests using the increased call center capacity.

Figure 3-7 provides an example of visualizing benefits and how various benefits can be arrayed and how they fit into more than type of category. For example, planned benefits can be categorized as (a) a tangible or intangible benefit, (b) a direct or indirect benefit, or (c) a combination of each of these categories.

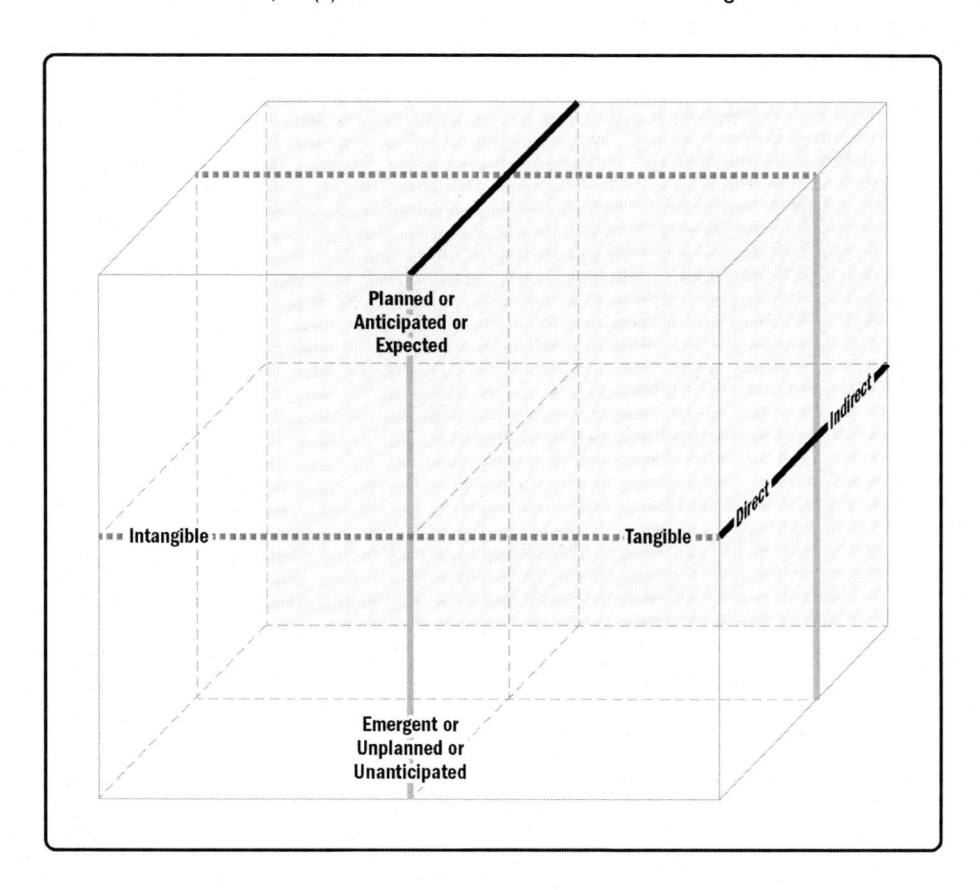

Figure 3-7. Benefits Categorization Cube

In addition to the benefit categories outlined previously, there is another category that can have a significant impact on benefits realization management. This is the category of disbenefits.

- **Disbenefits.** Disbenefits are a direct consequence of an output from a portfolio, program, or project that is perceived by one or more stakeholders as unfavorable. For example, a highway expansion program that aims to remove congestion between a major metropolitan area and its surrounding suburbs may look at funding options for the various road construction projects needed to get the projects scheduled in a shorter time. One option may be a public/private partnership relying on revenue sharing from a toll road option for the highway expansion. The benefit is the rapid construction of additional travel lanes, which would alleviate traffic congestion currently experienced by commuters. However, a disbenefit from this approach is the higher travel cost to commuters who choose to use dedicated toll lanes. If the toll road cost (disbenefit) from this solution is perceived as excessive, public support for the new highway expansion project may diminish. This could jeopardize the feasibility of the entire program, where the disbenefits outweigh the benefits.

    Disbenefits are real considerations and need to be factored effectively into all BRM decisions. The overall benefits of selected options, programs, and projects should outweigh any perceived disbenefits as they are identified.

    Disbenefits may also fall under other benefit types. As with benefits, disbenefits may be tangible or intangible, direct or indirect, or planned or emergent.

    Disbenefits deliver negative impacts to the initiative, whereas benefits are perceived as delivering positive impacts. The BRM strategy, benefits realization roadmap, and benefits realization plan need to address disbenefits in addition to benefits.

Classifying benefits by categories helps benefit stakeholders gain clarity into the pursued and planned benefits and disbenefits, against the other options being considered.

3.5.3.2 ADDITIONAL CATEGORIZATION

There are some additional categories that can help identify which stakeholder groups can be engaged in assessing and quantifying benefits. The following additional benefit categories are commonly cited examples:

- **Targeted stakeholder groups.** Benefits may be categorized by which stakeholder groups are impacted. The impact may be positive or negative. The key is to better understand how the groups are impacted and which groups should be engaged in helping to identify, quantify, and realize the benefits.
- **Financial benefits.** These benefits are those that can be monetized, as opposed to nonfinancial benefits, which generally cannot be monetized, except through proxy indicators. Examples of financial benefits are

those associated with an organization's reputation and its impact on gaining additional investment funding. Categorizing benefits as financial benefits aids the benefit owner in identifying specific measures or metrics for tracking delivery performance toward success. Financial benefits may be subcategorized as:

- *Sustainable/ongoing.* Financial gains from the benefit continue into the future, such as increased revenue;
- *One-off/discrete.* Financial gain from the benefit is a one-time occurrence, such as a one-time revenue or savings;
- *Cost avoidance.* Financial gain is a reduction in operating cost, avoidance of fines or penalties, or some other form of cost reduction to the organization; and
- *Capability improvement.* Financial gain is some form of operating efficiency, capability, or capacity factor.

◆ **Internal/external benefits.** Internal benefits are those affecting functional departments or groups internal to the organization. External benefits affect groups external to the organization, such as customers or the general public. Knowing whether the primary beneficiaries of a given benefit are internal or external to the performing organization helps the benefit owners and portfolio, program, and project managers better understand who is impacted by these delivery efforts. This identifies who should be appropriately engaged in decision making around issues affecting the delivery of a particular benefit.

◆ **Long-term/short-term benefits.** Long-term benefits are those that prepare the organization for future opportunities or challenges. Short-term benefits are those aimed at addressing current challenges or opportunities.

To successfully manage benefits realization, the timing as to when the benefits will be realized should take into account appropriate measures to track the progress toward attaining them.

Categorizing benefits being sought helps the organization understand how these benefits align with the strategic direction the organization is pursuing. Categorizing benefits also helps to prioritize benefits and identify which groups could be affected by the benefits. Increased understanding leads to better communication and effective engagement of different stakeholders. Each organization needs to identify sets of benefit categories to help them understand *how* and *why* the benefits are being pursued.

3.5.4 BENEFITS MEASUREMENT

Monitoring and measuring planned benefits span the whole length of the BRM life cycle. Regardless of the monitoring and measuring scheme, the critical question should be: Are we measuring things that tell us a planned benefit is still achievable during development, at delivery, and upon realization and sustainment? The benefit owner is accountable for the measurement scheme from business case through sustainment.

It is critical that measurement and evaluation methods be used across the BRM life cycle and be clearly specified in the approved business case. This is done in recognition of the need to establish a results-oriented mindset on the part of all participants.

Each benefit in the benefits realization management plan has a preliminary set of planned measurements. These measurements, however, imply flexibility and constant revalidation across the BRM life cycle. As appropriate, measurements can be modified with approval of the benefit owner.

Measurements vary by benefit type and the organization's preferences. From portfolio, program, and project perspectives, measurements fall into two broad categories: those before outputs are completed, and those after outputs are completed and transferred to beneficiaries of planned benefits.

The managers of portfolios, programs, and projects should develop designated measurements gauging the progress and alignment to plan. These measurements can be interim measurements or can be developed progressively according to the business case and benefits realization management plan. This includes incorporating emergent benefits during the BRM life cycle.

Measurements enable the evaluation of progress toward planned benefits, including conformance to strategic alignment and resources allocation and management. Measurements also help to define and manage achievement by identifying when completion has been reached. Measurements also identify when changes need to be made or when to terminate the investment if the planned outcomes and benefits are no longer aligned with strategy or cannot be achieved.

3.5.4.1 FACTORS INFLUENCING BENEFITS MEASUREMENT

Categorizing planned benefits helps an organization identify an appropriate measurement approach to track progress toward successful realization. Locally devised standards of the categories with appropriate measurements can aid the organization to set up a measurement system that can be adapted when new goals, with similar benefits, are identified for other programs and projects.

As noted in Section 3.5.3, there are several categories of benefits, but there are a few common ones that fit all situations. Each organization needs to devise its own measurements to support the realization of its planned benefits and satisfy the reporting requirements of the benefit owner.

BRM embraces and acknowledges the need for ownership of the measurement scheme, from the business case through sustainment. Benefit owners and/or sponsors are ultimately responsible for benefit measurement. Each benefit requires measures to be recorded and reported at predetermined times. This varies by both category of benefit and organization; many are difficult to measure. Some are qualitative and most can be quantified, others are tangible or intangible.

The managers of portfolios, programs, and projects should have designated measures for gauging the development of outputs that lead to benefits realization.

Each benefit at any portfolio, program, and project level and at any point in the life cycle toward delivery, can be labeled as (a) tangible or intangible, (b) planned or emergent (unplanned), and (c) direct or indirect in nature. Unfortunately, not every identifiable benefit can be measured quantitatively. Some may need to be measured using qualitative measures. Other benefits can only be achieved post-completion of the program or project and would need suitable measures to be put in place.

During development of portfolio, program, and project outputs, standard domain-relative measures should suffice, assuming there is good alignment with the benefits realization management plan. This assumes that the diligent monitoring and validation of work progress will help to achieve the eventual realization of planned benefits.

One doesn't always have to express something quantifiably to prove satisfactory knowledge and understanding or, in this case, benefits realization. For example, not all benefits could be planned or even measured for the Sydney Opera House, which was a major construction project in Australia. However, this does not negate the need or requirement to measure benefits. Benefits measurement strives to answer the question: "Given a benefit attempting to be realized, how will one know when this goal is attained?"

The Sydney Opera House may have had many tangible benefits, both during the construction and commissioning phases of delivery. But the enduring beauty and social impact it has achieved in the long term to the community, visitors, and the nation, was difficult to measure during the concept and planning phases, and difficult to imagine until years after completion. The functional measurement of seats sold during the years of ongoing programs of performances is an obvious, quantifiable indicator of realized benefits. However, the site of the unique building and the iconic nature of its significance to the country's presence in the world (national pride) is difficult to not only imagine at the concept stage, but is difficult to measure as the (clear) intangible and valuable benefit it now provides.

As an example, the following measures that may apply to benefits generated by organizations include:

- **Tangible**:
    - Return on investment (ROI),
    - Cost reduction/avoidance change,
    - Market share change, and
    - Increased revenue generation change.

- **Intangible:**
  - Employee morale,
  - Customer satisfaction,
  - Regulatory action avoidance, and
  - Brand or image perceptions.

Intangible benefits are often difficult to measure directly. Proxy measures are often used in these instances. A proxy measure is a measure that approximates of indirectly measures the benefit being sought. In measuring intangible benefits, benefit owners and/or sponsors need to select agreed-upon proxy measures for achievement. These may include surveys, polls, frequency of use indicators, and other qualitative measures of success or satisfaction that can stand in as an indirect measure for the benefit.

Table 3-1 illustrates a simple example of measurements assigned to different types of benefits, noting particularly the development period of deliverables from portfolios, programs, and projects. Table 3-2 illustrates an example of a variety of measures that may be used as a resource for organizations to use or develop for types of benefits.

Table 3-1. Brief Example of Benefit Measurements

Benefit Profile/ Benefit Number/ Name	Internal/ External Beneficiaries	Financial/ NonFinancial	Realization Horizon	Emergent Benefits Potential	Identify-Execute Stage BRM Metrics	Sustain Stage BRM Metrics
B-1. Function Z Productivity Enhancement	Internal	Financial	Short term	Low	Third-party internal assessment of business case and benefits realization management plan metrics, optimization, and stability of assumptions regarding costs, schedule, quality, risks, and strategic alignment	ROI, overtime reduction, time to business-as-usual
B-2. Customer Satisfaction Improvement Campaign	Internal External	Financial Nonfinancial	Long term	Medium	Third-party internal assessment of business case and benefits realization management plan metrics, optimization, and stability of assumptions regarding quality, schedule, costs, risks, and strategic alignment	Customer satisfaction improvement target, market share target, and revenue increase target

Table 3-2. Example Configuration of Benefits Measurement Resource

Measure	Scale (Example)	Tangible/ Intangible (T/I)	Notes	Direct/ Indirect (D/I)	Notes	Planned/ Emergent (P/E)	Notes
ROI	%	T	Can be calculated at each aspect of delivery program or strategy. Often associated with the requirements of a business case.	D	Needs close management if target is to be achieved. Unlikely to gain a positive improvement over target but can easily be a negative.	P	ROI is a planned target. Improvement unlikely through unplanned action.
Cost Reduction/ Avoidance	$, %	T	Targets are normally quantitative and either financial or stated as a percentage of an existing financial figure.	D/I	Needs close management if target is to be achieved. Unlikely to gain a positive improvement over target but can easily be a negative.	P	Unlikely cost reduction will be unplanned, but it is possible to improve during actual delivery.
Gain Market Share	%	T	This is a specific goal—either achieved or not (gain).	D/I	May change positive or negative through outside influences (competitors circumstances change) on this measure.	P/E	Unlikely cost-reduction will be unplanned, but it is possible to improve during actual delivery.
Employee Morale	Percent change or on a scale of 1 to 5	I	Whatever goal is set to be the target, it can easily change—generally lost more quickly than gained/improved.	D/I	May also be qualitative and, because of management changes, can have both a positive or negative impact on this measure.	P/E	Both a positive and a negative influenced by both planned and unplanned actions.
Customer Satisfaction	Percent change or on a scale of 1 to 5	I	As this is a specific target, it can easily change—generally goes down more quickly than it improves.	D/I	Can change as a direct/ indirect consequence of what competitors do and customer experiences.	P/E	May change during the delivery life cycle, either up or down.
Regulatory Action Avoidance	Yes or no to completion	I	This is a specific "should do" target and may carry both positive and negative changes/consequences.	D	Fixed target—should deliver as planned.	P	Only planned can be achieved as a fixed target. Emergent benefits that fall into this type of measure need to be more discretely planned to establish a fixed target type of measure to be monitored.
Other...							

Regardless of the metrics an organization uses, a key to benefits measurement is the recognition that the organization needs to put a system in place to allow monitoring of the progress being made toward benefits realization. These measurements provide information on progress and provide an opportunity to adjust approaches and plans. Another key is that the measurements put in place allow the benefit owners and key stakeholders to assess whether or not the benefits being sought are being—or can be—realized.

3.5.4.2 ROLES AND BENEFITS MEASUREMENT

There are several various roles (individual contributions) described in the literature relating to benefits measurement across the BRM life cycle. This includes strategic roles with oversight of processes (often associated with the benefit owners and/or sponsor), middle-level roles for benefits coordination and interpretation of data (most likely those associated with managing the actual delivery), and lower-level roles for the collection and analysis of data.

Benefit owners generally own the measurement methods and evaluation from start to finish of the delivery process. Managers of portfolios, programs, and projects may contribute to the definition of BRM measurement during the Identify life-cycle stage, particularly when these managers have prior experience. Benefit owners may delegate primary responsibility for specific measuring and evaluating progress toward benefits realization, with those closer to the delivery functions.

Recognizing that many stakeholders need to be involved alongside benefit owners and sponsors, the use of a matrix-based responsibility assignment matrix (RAM) or similar chart may be useful to define roles.

3.5.4.3 TIMING OF BENEFITS MEASUREMENT

While there is consensus that benefit measurement needs consideration from the inception of any program or project proposal, there is likely to be less agreement on the stage at which measurements should be planned and defined for monitoring purposes. Some sources of BRM guidance suggest this happens as a gradual process, with benefits first being identified as qualitative concepts and later being turned into measures for tracking.

For more tangible and predictable initiatives, metrics for measuring planned benefits should be defined in the benefits realization management plan. For more uncertain or iterative initiatives, such as software development or experimental R&D projects, a more gradual identification of measurements may be better. In any case, measurements typically are summarized for review and appropriate action by the benefit owner at regular review or phase-gate meetings. If emergent benefits arise, their management and measurement are integrated with the benefits management realization plan.

3.5.5 BENEFITS AND REQUIREMENT TRACEABILITY

The strategic objectives of an organization are subject to internal strengths and weaknesses (e.g., organizational project management (OPM), strategic execution maturity, and competence) and external opportunities and threats (e.g., partners, competitors, and other stakeholders) impacted by economic, social, and environmental contexts.

Leaders of organizations should ask questions such as the following:

- ◆ Given the strategic assessment, how can the organization survive adapting to the changing context?
- ◆ What happens if the organization continues business as usual without changing its strategies or action plans?
- ◆ How can the organization grow by leveraging strengths and opportunities, mitigating any threats, and reducing any weaknesses?
- ◆ How can the organization continually improve and innovate?

Each of these questions is required to be addressed if the organization is to succeed. Organizational leaders should initiate portfolios, programs, and projects in response to the questions and look for BRM to deliver positive results.

According to the *PMBOK® Guide*, there are four fundamental categories of initiating objectives that result in organizations chartering projects:

- ◆ To meet regulatory, legal, or social requirements linked to the survival objective (i.e., continue to operate);
- ◆ To satisfy stakeholder requests or growth needs;
- ◆ To implement or change business or technological strategies, addressing the business perpetuation objective; and
- ◆ To create, improve, or fix products, processes, or services to achieve a combination of the business objectives.

These organizational objectives are translated into requirements as a basis for scoping programs and projects, including service-level requirements for operational procedures.

Functional and nonfunctional requirements are derived from these needs and are sources of acceptance criteria for program and project outputs leading to benefits realization. Benefits are linked to business requirements of outputs or deliverables that enable the achievement of planned outcomes. Realized benefits create value, which is the net result of realized benefits less the cost of achieving them.

The value drivers are the factors that are likely to have the greatest impact on an organization's success; they are specific to different industries and companies. There are different categories of value drivers, for example types (such as growth drivers, operational drivers, or financial drivers) or levels (such as generic or business-unit specific levels).

When action is required to realize a specific value driver, for example, managing inventory turns or variables that affect working capital, the value driver should be defined at an explicit and commensurate level where action can be taken toward its realization.

Mapping value drivers helps to identify the benefits necessary to maximize an organization's value and justifies new portfolio components (programs and projects) or a continuation of those components in the Execution stage in their respective business cases. Figure 3-8 is an example of mapping value drivers.

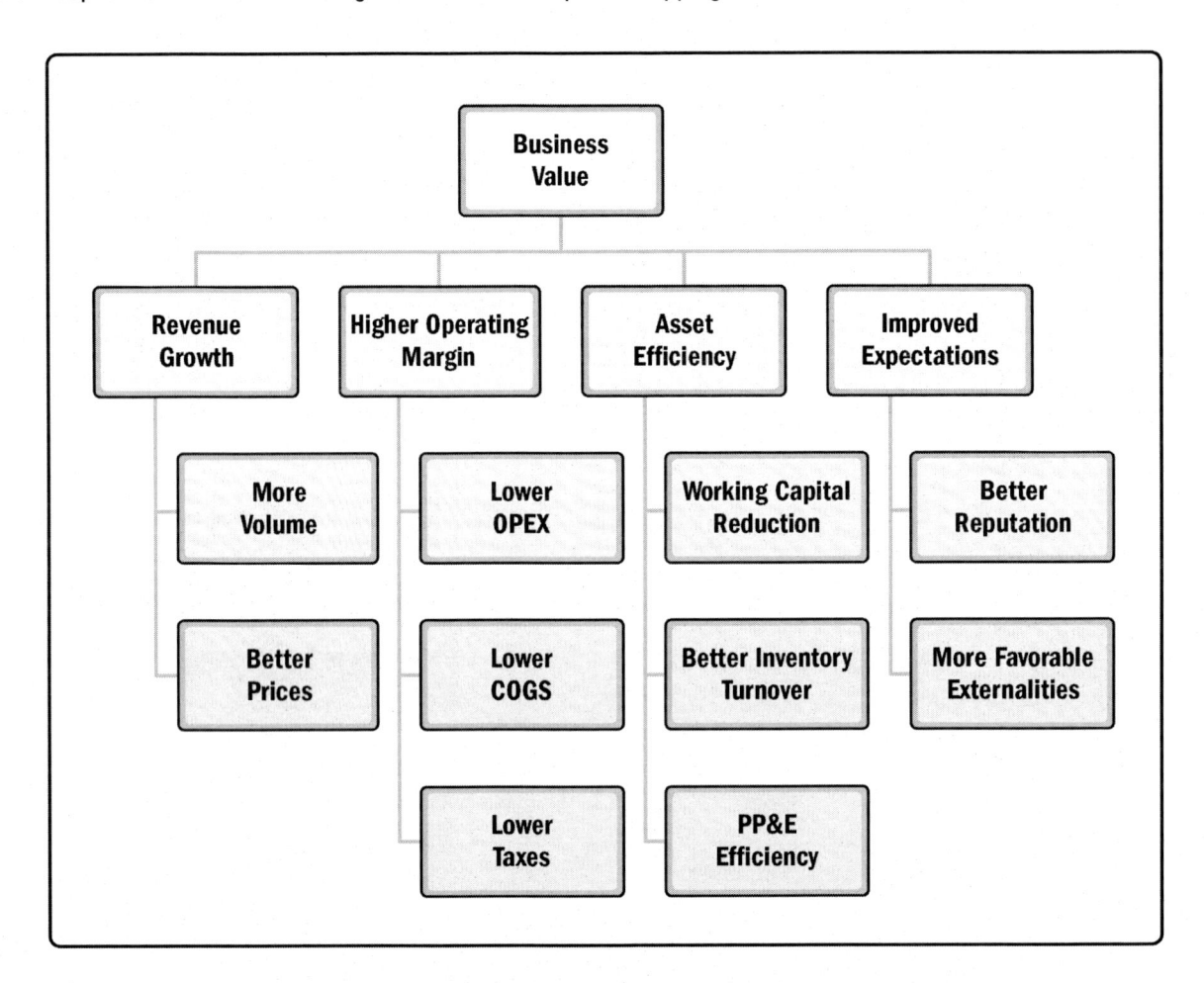

Figure 3-8. Example of Value Driver Map to Help Identify and Plan Benefits

The organization needs to consider the introduction of new value propositions or improve their existing business model. Mapping value drivers helps to identify and plan benefits that need to be defined, developed, and realized.

Such mapping drills down from organizational objectives to programs and projects and their respective business cases and benefits realization management plans.

The business case document provides the reasoning behind why an opportunity is to be explored, a problem is to be solved, or an obligation is to be complied with. To achieve any of these, the best viable and realizable options for the courses of action to be adopted need to be articulated.

The agreed business case and benefits realization management plan supporting the initiative become key to identifying requirements that should ensure successful delivery of outputs and realization of benefits. The outputs, in the form of solutions, products, or services, should be aligned with the right set of capabilities and describe how they will help to achieve the planned outcomes and realize the planned benefits. Effective requirements management is directly linked to the traceability of input resources and benefits achieved.

Requirements definition is enhanced by understanding alternative solutions, planned benefits, and other program requirements needed to improve the probability of success in program and project delivery.

The benefits traceability matrix is used to capture the mapping of specific portfolio, program, and project outputs to resulting benefits in line with and tied to the overarching organizational strategic goals. The benefits traceability matrix is used to record specific important parameters associated with benefits, such as categories, alignment, ownership, and associated projects. The benefits register is used for the ongoing management, tracking, and reporting of benefits realization at the portfolio, program, or project levels. The benefits register is maintained as the record of committed benefits and includes important information about planned benefits, actual benefits realized, related measures, timing, and project references.

4

GUIDANCE FOR PORTFOLIO, PROGRAM, AND PROJECT MANAGEMENT IN A BRM CONTEXT

4.1 OVERVIEW

Portfolios, programs, and projects create outputs that yield various types of outcomes resulting in benefits and value for the organization. BRM needs to be a consistent and visible part of the commonly accepted ways of managing them. This section provides general guidance for practitioners who want to learn or improve their roles as they pertain to BRM. First, consider basic definitions of portfolio, program, and project and their place in BRM.

Portfolio management is the centralized management of one or more portfolios to achieve strategic objectives. This centralization enables the organization to prioritize, for example, programs and projects with consideration for the relative importance of associated benefits. These priorities are reviewed across the BRM life cycle, where portfolio management decisions and actions help ensure realization as planned.

Programs are common elements of portfolios. Program management is the application of knowledge, skills, and principles to a program to achieve the program objectives and to obtain benefits and control not available by managing program components individually. Program managers lead delivering outputs of the program that yield the outcomes that enable associated benefits to be realized as planned.

Projects are temporary endeavors that are undertaken to create unique products, services, or results. This definition is applicable regardless of whether projects are managed independently, directly as part of a portfolio, or as part of a program. Benefits are realized as the project's outputs are used, resulting in the outcomes that result in the benefits being realized. The challenge is to keep project work, from beginning to end, aligned with the business case and benefits realization management plan.

Although actual realization of benefits depends on the creation and transfer of portfolio, program, and project outputs (or deliverables), emergent benefits and disbenefits may appear during the Execute and Sustain stages. The benefit owner is responsible and accountable for managing benefits throughout the entire BRM life cycle, including when work is underway through portfolios, programs, and projects.

This practice guide assumes that organizations use three principal means of developing and delivering outputs that lead to benefits realization: portfolios, programs, and projects. Organizations that recognize only projects should consider tailoring the principles and practices outlined in this guide for their specific use. For example, if the organization does not practice formal portfolio management and has only projects, as in many small-to-medium entities, project managers should interface directly with the senior leader responsible for the planned outcomes and benefits that project outputs should generate.

For reference, Figure 4-1 shows the approximate engagement durations of portfolios, programs, and projects. These durations may vary by organization.

Sections 4.2 through 4.5 focus on guidance to be effective with BRM in the roles of the portfolio, program, and project manager, in addition to the business analyst. While each of the PMI foundational standards have addressed BRM to various degrees, the purpose here is to have a compilation of appropriate role activities across the BRM life cycle.

Identify Stage
1. Develop business case and benefits realization management plan
2. Authorize and charter

Execute Stage
3. Develop outputs - optimize benefits
4. Deliver outputs and transfer ownership

Sustain Stage
5. Realize benefits
6. Adapt benefits

Project Management Life Cycle
Starting-Organizing-Doing Work-Closing

Outcomes and Benefits Realized by Operations and Other Internal/External Beneficiaries and Stakeholders

Program Management Life Cycle
Definition-Delivery-Closure

Portfolio Management Duration—Life Cycle
Initiation-Planning-Execution-Optimization

BRM LIFE CYCLE DURATION

Monitor, Measure, Evaluate, and Report per Benefits Realization Management Plan(s)

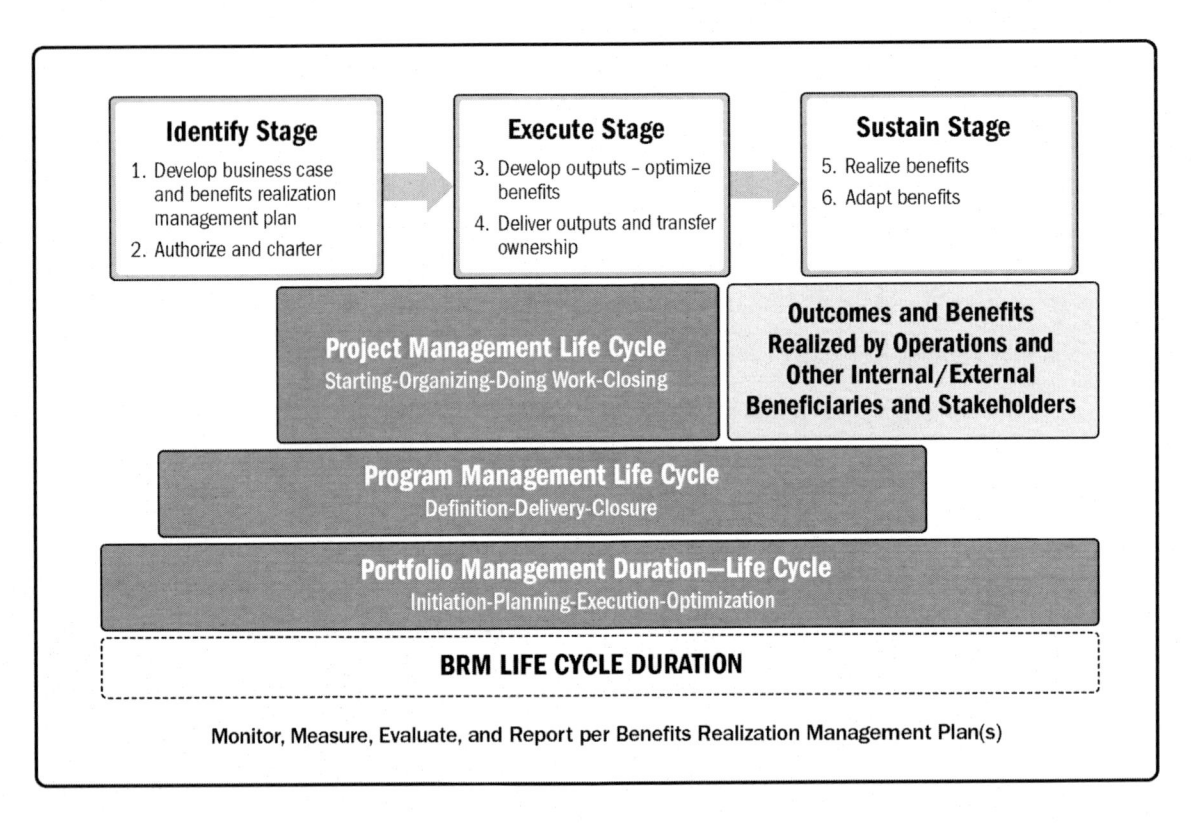

Figure 4-1. Portfolio-Program and Project Life Cycles in BRM Context

4.2 BRM GENERAL GUIDANCE FOR PORTFOLIO MANAGERS

While there are multiple and dynamic aspects that portfolio managers should address (see *The Standard for Portfolio Management* [9]), the BRM element starts with understanding the relationship of the portfolio management life cycle to the BRM life cycle, as shown in Figure 4-1. Portfolio management essentially spans to BRM life cycle.

The BRM life cycle applies to each authorized benefit. There may be multiple planned benefits identified in the portfolio at any given time. Portfolio managers with their governing bodies support the organization's BRM practices during the portfolio's operational lifetime by taking actions such as:

◆ Diligently follow BRM and portfolio management policies, plans, measures, and practices, and require components to do the same;

◆ Practice prioritization of higher-value planned benefits with the strongest strategic intent;

◆ Ensure continuous alignment of portfolio components to approved strategy and planned benefits;

◆ Balance and optimize potential benefits, risks, and resources;

◆ Create a benefits register to begin the process of identifying benefits to be tracked in the portfolio;

◆ Monitor benefits realization potential based on component progress measures;

◆ Watch for *cancel conditions* where costs negate the planned benefit and related value;

◆ Proactively track and analyze performance of the portfolio and look for any indication of bottlenecks, systemic issues, and capacity constraints that impede the realization of planned benefits;

◆ Facilitate discussions with stakeholders to help ensure the realization of planned benefits;

◆ Facilitate transfer of component outputs into planned outcomes and realized benefits by beneficiaries;

◆ Facilitate measurement of benefits and corresponding actions for the sustainment stage; and

◆ Champion adoption of appropriate practices that work for the organization, along with pertinent lessons from successful practices around BRM and portfolio management.

Benefits within the portfolio should be defined in the benefits register at a high level, in keeping with the theme or category of the portfolio, by capturing how each component's performance contributes to the portfolio's overall value to the organization. These benefits should be directly related to planned benefits, which are defined in more detail at the program level.

4.3 BRM GENERAL GUIDANCE FOR PROGRAM MANAGERS

Programs are mainstays for generating collective outputs that lead to planned outcomes and benefits (see Figure 4-1 in *The Standard for Program Management*) [10] The high-level relationship of the program life cycle to BRM is shown in Figure 4-1 of this practice guide.

The following information is intended as guidance for program managers engaged with the BRM life cycle stages. Its intent is to heighten awareness of planned and emergent benefits—not to replace any normal program manager roles and responsibilities.

- ◆ **When participating in the BRM Identify stage:**
    - Assist as appropriate with identification and qualification of benefits.
    - Contribute appropriate topical knowledge to development of the business case and benefits realization management plan.
    - Ascertain the benefit owner's and other stakeholders' expectations.
    - Collaborate with the assigned business analyst.
    - Lead collaboratively with the benefit owner in completion of a robust benefits realization management plan.

- ◆ **When participating in the BRM Execute stage:**
    - Ensure the benefit owner and the rest of the program team are engaged with an agreed-upon program communications plan that emphasizes alignment of program work to planned benefits and relevant metrics.
    - Facilitate the use of the benefits realization management plan with the program team.
    - Map critical elements of the program management plan to the benefits realization management plan.
    - Review and revalidate planned work to planned benefits at kickoff, phase-gate, or other regular program meetings.
    - Alert the program team to detection and reporting of emergent benefits.
    - Monitor and report component progress in light of planned benefits.
    - Maintain the program benefits register.
    - At project closeouts, capture and convey pertinent BRM lessons learned.

- ◆ **When participating in the BRM Sustain stage:**
    - Consolidate output transfers and implementation plans and measures, as appropriate, consistent with the benefits realization management plans.

- Assist with the transfer of the ongoing responsibility for supporting the corresponding outcomes required for ongoing delivery of benefits.
- Monitor performance of benefits, as appropriate, with the benefit owner.

4.4 BRM GENERAL GUIDANCE FOR PROJECT MANAGERS

Project managers have a frontline role in producing the outputs that contribute to planned outcomes and planned benefits. Project work tends to be concentrated in the Execute BRM life cycle stage as shown in Figure 4-1.

The following information is intended as guidance for project managers engaged with BRM. Its intent is to heighten awareness of planned and emergent benefits—not to replace any normal project manager roles and responsibilities.

- **When participating in the BRM Identify stage:**
  - Contribute to the development of the business case and benefits realization management plan.
  - Ascertain the benefit owner and other stakeholders' expectations.
  - Collaborate with the program manager and assigned business analyst, as appropriate.
- **When participating in the BRM Execute stage:**
  - Ensure the benefit owner and the program manager, as appropriate, are engaged with an agreed-to communication plan that emphasizes alignment of project work to outputs leading to planned benefits, as well as alignment to relevant BRM metrics.
  - Obtain and incorporate the benefits realization management plan with the project plan and share with the project team and other stakeholders.
  - Map the critical elements of the project management plan to the benefits realization management plan.
  - Review and revalidate planned work to planned benefits at kickoff, phase-gate, or other regular project meetings.
  - Alert the project team to detection and reporting of emergent benefits.
  - At project closeout, capture and convey pertinent BRM lessons learned.
- **When participating in the BRM Sustain stage:**
  - Assist the benefit owner with transfer and implementation plans and measures, as appropriate, consistent with the benefits realization management plan.

4.5 BRM GENERAL GUIDANCE FOR BUSINESS ANALYSTS

Business analysts have a direct role in identifying business needs and in defining planned benefits. Business analysts perform activities to support the delivery of the outputs leading to outcomes or solutions that align with strategic objectives. With participation across much, if not all, of the BRM life cycle, business analysts follow this general guidance during each stage:

- **When participating in the BRM Identify stage:**
  - Determine the defined, potential benefits that should arise from implementing targeted outputs to solve problems and attain opportunities commensurate with the strategic objectives of the organization.
  - Seek outputs leading to broader solutions for business requirements that deliver value.
  - Collaborate with portfolio, program, and project managers and other stakeholders to identify the benefits being sought and develop a sound business case to justify the efforts necessary to realize these benefits.

- **When participating in the BRM Execute stage:**
  - Work with applicable stakeholders to identify all product requirements necessary to achieve the outputs for the outcomes and benefits being sought.
  - Ensure the outputs lead to realization of intended benefits through appropriate monitoring and measurement.
  - Alert portfolio, program, and project teams and benefit owners when it seems the outputs might not deliver the benefits.

- **When participating in the BRM Sustain stage:**
  - Aid in product evaluation efforts to help ensure the delivered outputs provide intended outcomes and realized benefits of continuous value for beneficiaries.
  - Monitor whether outcomes and realized benefits meet the need and expectations of the beneficiaries and other stakeholders for which strategic initiatives were undertaken.

APPENDIX X1
CONTRIBUTORS AND REVIEWERS OF
BENEFITS REALIZATION MANAGEMENT: A PRACTICE GUIDE

The Project Management Institute is grateful to all of these individuals for their support and acknowledges their contributions to the project management profession.

X1.1 BRM CORE COMMITTEE

The following individuals served as members, were contributors of text or concepts, and served as leaders within the Project Core Committee:

    Farhad Abdollahyan, PMP, PMI-RMP
    Michael Joseph Frenette PMP, SMC
    Mustafa Hafizoglu, MSc, PMP
    Kindra Howard, PMP, BRMP
    Paul E. Shaltry, MA, PMP
    Chris Stevens, PhD
    Dave Violette, MPM, PMP
    Lorna Scheel, MSc, PMI Standards Compliance Specialist
    Ashley Wolski, MBA, Standards Project Specialist

X1.2 SME REVIEWERS

In addition to the Committee, the following individuals provided their review and recommendations for this practice guide:

Imad Alsadeq, MSc, MSP, PMP
Amgad Badewi, PhD, PMP
Greta Blash, PMP, PMI-PBA
Peter Berndt de Souza Mello, PMP, PMI-SP
Farid F. Bouges, PhD, PfMP, PMP
Richard Breese, MA, DBA
Cyndi Dionisio, PMP, PMI-ACP
Vick Ekizian, PMI-RMP
Iain Fraser, PMP, PMI Fellow
Patrick Girard, MSc, PMP
Ruth Anne Guerrero, MBA, PMP
Nagy Hamamo, PMP, Managing Benefits Practitioner
Mohammad Ichsan, PhD, PMP, PMI-SP
Steve Jenner, FCMA, MBA
Mark Kennedy, PMP
Kevin Korterud,
Aries Nagy, PMP
Marvin R. Nelson, MBA, SCPM
Eric S. Norman, PgMP, PMI Fellow
Deena Gordon Parla, PMP
Crispin "Kik" Piney, BSc, PgMP
Carlos Eduardo Martins Serra, MSc, PMP
David W. Ross, PgMP, PMP
Morten Sorensen, PfMP, PgMP
Langeswaran Supramaniam, MSc, BEng (Hons), PMP
John Thorp, CMC, ISP
Stephen A. Townsend
Merv Wyeth, MA (Exon), FAPM

X1.3 PMI STANDARDS PROGRAM MEMBER ADVISORY GROUP (MAG)

The following individuals served as members of the PMI Standards Program Member Advisory Group during development of the practice guide:

Maria Cristina Barbero, PMI-ACP, PMP, CSM
Brian Grafsgaard, PfMP, PgMP, PMP, CSM
David Gunner, MSc, PMP, PfMP
Hagit Landman, PMP, PMI-SP, MBA
Vanina Mangano, PMP
Yvan Petit, PhD, MEng, MBA, PMP, PfMP
John Zlockie, MBA. PMP, PMI Standards Manager

X1.4 PRODUCTION STAFF

Special mention is due to the following employees of PMI:

    Donn Greenberg, Manager, Publications
    Roberta Storer, Product Editor
    Barbara Walsh, Publications Production Supervisor
    Kim Shinners, Publications Associate

APPENDIX X2
BENEFITS REALIZATION MANAGEMENT READINESS SURVEY

This survey is intended to help an organization perform a self-assessment of where it stands relative to important implementation factors related to benefits realization management (BRM). The survey is designed for organizations either launching or upgrading their BRM programs. It is intended to help organizations assess how well they have embraced and embedded the BRM principles and critical success enablers (CSEs) into their respective cultures and practices.

BRM principles guide the behaviors, thinking, and decision making of benefit owners, senior business leaders, and other stakeholders. The same principles extend to beneficiaries, in addition to portfolio, program, and project managers and their teams. CSEs are those organizational capabilities that contribute to the effectiveness and efficiency of BRM. An essential purpose of CSEs is their ability to prepare the organization to achieve expected (planned) outcomes and benefits. Having the correct CSEs in place helps an organization to manage their portfolios, programs, and projects for the purpose of delivering outputs that yield outcomes creating benefits.

This survey is best used by collecting input for the assessment from the organizational roles involved in BRM such as:

- Executive leadership;
- Operational/functional management;
- Benefit owners;
- Portfolio, program, and project managers;
- Business analysts; and
- Other roles within the organization involved in managing or leading initiatives for attaining benefits.

The survey can also be used selectively to gather input from key members of the organization or, holistically, to gain broad input from across the organization.

This survey has two sections. The first focuses on the core principles of BRM. The second addresses CSEs.

The results of the survey should be combined into an aggregate assessment of organizational readiness and made available for key decision leaders in the organization. The leaders can assess the strengths and weaknesses of the organization against the BRM principles and critical success factors to identify action plans to attain critical alignment with these principles and critical success enablers.

X2.1 CORE PRINCIPLES OF BRM

For each of the five core principles identified in Sections X2.1.1 through X2.1.5, select the rating that matches how much you agree that your organization fully embraces the principle.

X2.1.1 NET BENEFITS JUSTIFY THE USE OF INVESTED RESOURCES (TABLE X2-1)

Outcomes deliver benefits against funded investments made in pursuit of the organization's strategic goals and business objectives, for which management of the portfolio, program, or project is undertaken.

- **Rationale.** Net planned benefits are what justifies the sponsoring organization to use valuable resources on the effort. Value needs to take into account the benefits and also the investment in the resources required to realize benefits.
- **Supporting artifacts.** Documentation of the efficacy of all planned and actual benefits with costs to achieve them, including the analysis of the net value received from the benefits.

Table X2-1. Principle: Net Benefits Justify the Use of Invested Resources

PRINCIPLE: NET BENEFITS JUSTIFY THE USE OF INVESTED RESOURCES				
How much do you agree your organization has fully embraced this principle?				
Strongly Disagree	Disagree	Neither Agree/Disagree	Agree	Strongly Agree
0	1	3	4	5

X2.1.2 COMMENCEMENT OF WORK IS DRIVEN BY BENEFITS IDENTIFICATION (TABLE X2-2)

Planned benefits during development and after delivery of outputs require clear identification *before* the work commences. These benefits should be unambiguously articulated to all delivery stakeholders and beneficiaries.

- **Rationale.** Delivering the expected value from planned benefits is what guides the thinking and decision making about the work to be undertaken. The value derived from benefits management should be clearly articulated, so all decision makers are able to make informed decisions regarding the work to be undertaken to eventually realize planned benefits.

- **Supporting artifacts.** Approved business case with benefits realization plan; regular reviews at phases or gates, and benefit forecasts or assessments.

Table X2-2. Principle: Commencement of Work Is Driven by Benefits Identification

PRINCIPLE: COMMENCEMENT OF WORK IS DRIVEN BY BENEFITS IDENTIFICATION				
How much do you agree your organization has fully embraced this principle?				
Strongly Disagree	Disagree	Neither Agree/Disagree	Agree	Strongly Agree
0	1	3	4	5

X2.1.3 PLANNED BENEFITS ARE IDENTIFIED IN AUTHORIZING DOCUMENTS (TABLE X2-3)

All planned benefits should be appraised, estimated, verified, and agreed by the organization, key stakeholders, and appropriate beneficiaries in an authorizing document (business case, benefits management realization plan, and portfolio/program/project charter). These benefits are monitored and managed as part of the portfolio, program, and project management life cycles.

- **Rationale.** To effectively appraise, formally document, monitor, and measure planned outcomes and benefits. This enables the organization to effectively monitor progress toward achieving those planned benefits.

- **Supporting artifacts.** Business case, charter, benefits register, benefit profile, and documentation of updates.

Table X2-3. Principle: Planned Benefits Are Identified in Authorizing Documents

PRINCIPLE: PLANNED BENEFITS ARE IDENTIFIED IN AUTHORIZING DOCUMENTS				
How much do you agree your organization has fully embraced this principle?				
Strongly Disagree	Disagree	Neither Agree/Disagree	Agree	Strongly Agree
0	1	3	4	5

X2.1.4 BENEFITS REALIZATION IS HOLISTICALLY PLANNED AND MANAGED (TABLE X2-4)

Benefits realization is considered holistically, planned and managed from the organization's perspective of needs and requirements, and not limited to those of the portfolio, program, or project delivery.

- ◆ **Rationale.** BRM extends beyond the portfolio, program, and project domains to the entire enterprise. For BRM to be successful, a broader, holistic perspective of the sponsoring organization should be built into the overall planning approach. This reduces the likelihood of shortcomings that may stem from the narrower focus of delivering only outputs through portfolio, program, and project management efforts. A holistic approach also includes taking unexpected changes into account, with opportunities and threats for benefits realization aligned to organizational goals.

- ◆ **Supporting artifacts.** Benefits traceability matrix, value/benefit mapping to balanced scorecards, or other strategic objective hierarchy, at the portfolio level.

Table X2-4. Principle: Benefits Realization Is Holistically Planned and Managed

PRINCIPLE: BENEFITS REALIZATION IS HOLISTICALLY PLANNED AND MANAGED				
How much do you agree your organization has fully embraced this principle?				
Strongly Disagree	Disagree	Neither Agree/Disagree	Agree	Strongly Agree
0	1	3	4	5

X2.1.5 GOVERNANCE AND ADEQUATE RESOURCES ARE ESSENTIAL TO BRM SUCCESS (TABLE X2-5)

BRM requires adequately provisioned resources, working within a clear governance structure with those responsible for managing and achieving the agreed outcomes being identified correctly as accountable and authorized to do so.

- ◆ **Rationale.** Organizations should invest resources and effort to realize and sustain benefits. In addition, organizations should invest in the appropriate level of resources. Organizations should provide a clear and adequate governance structure. They should give authority to appropriate individuals and hold them accountable for overall success.

- ◆ **Supporting artifacts.** Documented, current, approved benefit governance roles and responsibilities; responsibility matrix against the benefit register.

Table X2-5. Principle: Governance and Adequate Resources Are Essential to BRM Success

PRINCIPLE: GOVERNANCE AND ADEQUATE RESOURCES ARE ESSENTIAL TO BRM SUCCESS				
How much do you agree your organization has fully embraced this principle?				
Strongly Disagree	Disagree	Neither Agree/Disagree	Agree	Strongly Agree
0	1	3	4	5

X2.2 BRM CRITICAL SUCCESS ENABLERS (CSEs)

For each of the six critical success enablers identified in Sections X2.2.1 through X2.2.6, select the rating that matches how much you agree that your organization has fully established that CSE.

X2.2.1 ESTABLISH CLEAR BRM ROLES AND RESPONSIBILITIES (TABLE X2-6)

A key to successful BRM is the need for assigned benefit owners or sponsors and other involved leaders to be aligned with the organization's governance structure and BRM strategy. These roles have the accountability and responsibility to lead across the BRM life cycle, which is the management of a benefit from conception through realization and sustainment, expressed in the generic stages of Identify, Execute, and Sustain. Other senior leaders may be responsible to help manage change associated with reaching and realizing planned benefits, which are vital for ensuring overall portfolio, program, and project success. The use of RACI charts or similar techniques is a key way of clearly identifying accountabilities and responsibilities for key roles. These roles need visibility and insight into the programs and projects, and how strategic alignment, objectives, and related benefits are delivered. Benefit owners with the right insight provide the broad-view perspective and guide the overall portfolios, programs, and projects to better address the strategic intent of the planned benefits.

BRM helps to create visibility and insight regarding strategy and highlights deviations between program/project outputs and planned outcomes. This insight provides benefit owners the opportunity to make corrections where small changes can make a big difference. BRM also ensures executives can make decisions to support those programs and projects that directly link to the strategy. Benefit owners, sponsors, and other senior leaders can support BRM by reinforcing accountabilities throughout the associated portfolios, programs, and projects and by serving as role models for positive BRM behaviors.

◆ **Supporting artifacts.** Descriptions or roles and responsibilities for benefit definition, assessment, monitoring, control, and reporting, either in stand-alone documents or as part of organizational project management documents.

Table X2-6. CSE: Clear BRM Roles and Responsibilities Are Established

CSE: CLEAR BRM ROLES AND RESPONSIBILITIES ARE ESTABLISHED				
How much do you agree your organization has fully established this CSE?				
Strongly Disagree	Disagree	Neither Agree/Disagree	Agree	Strongly Agree
0	1	3	4	5

X2.2.2 DEVELOP THE RIGHT BRM CULTURE (TABLE X2-7)

Every organization profits by encouraging and reinforcing the adoption of BRM concepts, terminology, and processes across the portfolios, programs, and projects they commission. This enables the organization to build a BRM culture where executives, initiative leaders, suppliers, individual contributors, and stakeholders are able to easily identify and observe the intended outcomes, results, and benefits that are critical to each initiative's success.

The attributes of a BRM culture may include:

◆ Incorporating benefits formally in every business case, benefits realization management plan, and other initiating tool such as charters;

◆ Assessing portfolios, programs, and projects to ensure they align with strategic organizational objectives, targets, and planned benefits;

- Focusing on both tangible and intangible benefits, in addition to any related foreseen risks, and their relationship to success;
- Establishing appropriate levels of governance, with active engagement and shared responsibility among senior executives, those who identify targeted benefits for the sponsored programs and projects, and the managers who lead the delivery of realizing those planned benefits;
- Ensuring decision making related to benefits realization is characterized by effective, holistic problem solving;
- Encouraging initiative leaders to raise and prioritize issues that affect benefits realization early; and
- Demonstrating through behaviors and words, an awareness of how the organizational culture can positively or negatively impact planned benefits.

Conversely, there are some organizational attributes that can prevent the successful engagement of BRM within an organization. These should be avoided and discouraged, including:

- Punishing leaders and team members who share real initiative problems and issues;
- Focusing on staying on schedule regardless of impact to cost, quality, benefits, outcome, or result; and
- Ambiguous or poor communications that withhold important information.

To achieve success, leaders should encourage behaviors that create the organizational culture, inspiring and improving performance across the organization. BRM is a critical enabler to this success for the senior executives; business owners; and portfolio, program, and project leaders.

- **Supporting artifacts.** Portfolio, program, and project reports containing sections on benefits, governance board meeting agendas and reports with substantive consideration of benefits, reviews of business cases, and benefits realization plans.

Table X2-7. CSE: Right BRM Culture Is Developed

CSE: RIGHT BRM CULTURE IS DEVELOPED				
How much do you agree your organization has fully established this CSE?				
Strongly Disagree	Disagree	Neither Agree/Disagree	Agree	Strongly Agree
0	1	3	4	5

X2.2.3 BUILD THE RIGHT SKILL SETS (TABLE X2-8)

Developing skills to support BRM leads to a greater likelihood for success and improved achievement of planned benefits. BRM involves a variety of roles (see Section 2.2) with levels of engagement that can be clustered into four groups of skill sets:

- ◆ **Governance roles.** Governance roles include executives, senior management, leadership, and sponsors. Decision-making capabilities, leadership skills, and business acumen are needed to perform the governance roles associated with BRM. In addition to these generalized senior management skills, additional, more specific skills are necessary to enable senior leaders to:
    - Design and validate the governance roles, responsibilities, and governance body configuration;
    - Establish benefits management criteria, metrics to be monitored, and measurement parameters;
    - Review and approve benefits realization management plans;
    - Evaluate and approve chartering documents;
    - Assess performance against benefits realization criteria and measures at planned intervals;
    - Monitor, report, and publish progress against benefit targets for review by all levels of the organization; and
    - Identify and make changes to portfolio components (e.g., programs, projects, and operations) to achieve and sustain planned benefits.

    Additional guidance on establishing effective governance for portfolios, programs, and projects can be found in *Governance of Portfolios, Programs, and Projects: A Practice Guide* [5]. Further guidance on developing portfolio, program, and project manager competence can be found in *Project Manager Competency Development Framework – Third Edition* [6].

- ◆ **Stakeholder roles.** Stakeholder roles include middle management, operational management, and/or benefit owners, sponsors, and beneficiaries. These roles are performed by either (a) clients of the benefits being sought or (b) suppliers of resources and capabilities needed to create the outputs and outcomes necessary for realization of the benefits. These stakeholders have a very active role in the Identify stage of the BRM life cycle and should be able to:
    - Identify initiatives that can lead to the realization of the strategic benefits from a bottom up perspective;
    - Understand the value-for-money considerations in order to validate benefit profiles;
    - Aid in the development, appraisal, and approval of value/benefit maps;
    - Validate benefit measurement baselines and targets; and
    - Give input to transition plans and lessons learned reviews as lessons are learned and periodically reviewed throughout the initiative.

◆ **Managerial roles.** Managerial roles include benefits, portfolio, program, project, and change managers. These roles are responsible for managing the contribution of their area of expertise to the overall benefits, throughout the BRM life cycle. These roles report to governance roles and interact with stakeholders and specialist roles.

Organizational project management capabilities as defined in *Project Manager's Competency Development Framework (PMCDF)* [6] apply to these roles.

According to *Managing Change in Organizations: A Practice Guide* [7], successful change management provides organizations with a competitive advantage. A few critical success factors for successful change management (also referred to as organizational change management (OCM)) are: effective communication, addressing potential resistance, team collaboration, and the active support of the sponsor.

◆ **Specialist roles.** Specialist roles include benefits/business analysis. The skill set of benefits/business analysis comprises (a) analyzing and interpreting complex organizational data; (b) identifying problems and opportunities, (c) providing possible solutions that would yield benefits; and (d) developing dashboards, reports, and presentations. In addition to these skill sets, the roles need excellent communication skills with the ability to interact with and influence a wide range of leadership roles; senior stakeholders; and portfolio, program, project, and change managers. More specifically those engaged in benefit/business analysis should be able to:

- Facilitate workshops with governance, stakeholders, and managers to identify and select benefits and to develop specific measures and mechanisms for measuring benefits;
- Create a benefits traceability matrix or a benefits map showing the relationships between planned benefits and their enabling outcomes, capabilities, and initiatives;
- Review portfolio, program, and project charters against these initiative outputs and outcomes in their business case and benefits realization management plan to confirm their continuing alignment with business needs and expectations; Assess at regular intervals whether the benefits defined in the business case, benefits realization management plan, and initiative charter as captured in the benefits map are being realized by the operations/beneficiaries; and
- Support portfolio, program, project and change managers to ensure that all plans, outputs, and outcomes are aligned to the planned benefits.

◆ **Supporting artifacts.** BRM-oriented training programs with attendee participation and achievement noted.

Table X2-8. CSE: The Right Skill Sets Are Developed

CSE: THE RIGHT SKILL SETS ARE DEVELOPED				
How much do you agree your organization has fully established this CSE?				
Strongly Disagree	Disagree	Neither Agree/Disagree	Agree	Strongly Agree
0	1	3	4	5

X2.2.4 EMBRACE FLEXIBILITY (TABLE X2-9)

Organizations that tend to be good at BRM embrace flexibility, because in dynamic and changing environments, few programs or projects are delivered as originally planned. This implies that either BRM may not deliver the planned benefits or that expectations change during the delivery timeline. As the delivery environment changes, the benefits being sought may also need to be changed/adapted.

For example, when managing the benefits of an asset-value project/initiative, such as a construction project, the planned timeline is generally long and subject to the unexpected changes in external environmental economics, which are out of the control of those involved in the physical delivery. The original list of planned benefits captured in the benefits register or map may change; therefore, the list needs to change and be adapted to the new situation.

◆ **Supporting artifacts.** Change control process logs and requests including benefit management considerations.

Table X2-9. CSE: Flexibility Is Embraced

CSE: FLEXIBILITY IS EMBRACED				
How much do you agree your organization has fully established this CSE?				
Strongly Disagree	Disagree	Neither Agree/Disagree	Agree	Strongly Agree
0	1	3	4	5

X2.2.5 STRENGTHEN GOVERNANCE AND RISK MANAGEMENT (TABLE X2-10)

All portfolios of programs and projects pose a degree of risk. Risks can range from discrete risks that only affect a given program or project to overall risks that can affect the portfolio and the organization itself. Efforts undertaken by an organization to deliver the benefits being sought can also bring disbenefits to the organization or other beneficiaries. Identification of key risks and appropriate governance structures are essential to ensure that the delivery of programs and projects remains credible, appropriate, and useful in achieving planned benefits for the beneficiaries. Once a program or project is closed and the associated risk register is updated, any residual risks are moved to the next higher level in the governance structure for further monitoring or follow-up.

BRM can be embedded into existing governance structures for portfolios, programs, and projects where they may already exist. When BRM is not already embedded in these governance structures, steps should be taken to ensure BRM is part of the governance of portfolios, programs, and projects. This is key to ensuring benefits and value are being pursued and remain aligned with the organization's overall strategy. BRM provides the necessary monitoring and management mechanisms to track whether the benefits are actually realized. The governance structures also need to provide a way of ensuring benefits are sustained after program and project completion. These structures should also ensure adequate BRM metrics are available to monitor both tangible and intangible benefits, which are viewed as an integral part of ongoing portfolio, program, and project governance.

- ◆ **Supporting artifacts.** Governance documentation requires benefits to be considered as a parameter for impact assessment. This is in addition to scope, schedule, quality, cost, and other specific application area parameters including risk evaluation reports specifically addressing the risk impacts to benefits.

Table X2-10. CSE: Governance and Risk Management Are Strengthened

CSE: GOVERNANCE AND RISK MANAGEMENT ARE STRENGTHENED				
How much do you agree your organization has fully established this CSE?				
Strongly Disagree	Disagree	Neither Agree/Disagree	Agree	Strongly Agree
0	1	3	4	5

X2.2.6 ESTABLISH BENEFITS TRACKING (TABLE X2-11)

Benefits tracking involves identifying appropriate BRM metrics for use in effective management and leadership. This is essential to achieve the outputs and outcomes of the portfolios, programs, and projects in addition to the benefits for the beneficiaries. BRM metrics need to address both tangible and intangible benefits as applicable. This allows the tracking of progress toward benefits realization. BRM metrics are not required to be precise or holistic, but they should be viewed as essential to providing insight into trends and allowing a degree of forecasting for successful realization. Such forecasting is indicative of outcomes, and when necessary, can help improve portfolio, program, and project initiatives to help ensure benefits realization.

Appropriate, measurable, and an understood set of BRM metrics should be in place early to enable adequate monitoring. The measurement of benefits and their associated value as it materializes before, during, and after realization is critical to successful BRM.

- ◆ **Supporting artifacts.** Documentation and documented use of an approved monitoring and evaluation process for each benefit.

Table X2-11. CSE: Benefits Tracking Established

CSE: BENEFITS TRACKING ESTABLISHED				
How much do you agree your organization has fully established this CSE?				
Strongly Disagree	Disagree	Neither Agree/Disagree	Agree	Strongly Agree
0	1	3	4	5

APPENDIX X3
BRM RESEARCH SUMMARY

PMI commissioned two pieces of research by some of the world's leading thinkers and knowledge sources on benefits management/benefits realization. The aim was to aid and provide foresight and understanding for the development of this practice guide.

The first study provided a unified view of benefits management/benefits realization management to be integrated into PMI standards' and the second study looked at measures for benefits realization.

This appendix provides a summary of those two bodies of work.

X3.1 REPORT #1

X3.1.1 PURPOSE OF REPORT #1

Report #1 was based on the following four questions:

1. What is meant by benefits realization and benefits realization management?

2. Are there synonyms for benefits realization and benefits realization management? Which of these are used in academic research, either in an empirical or conceptual manner? Which are used in the consulting literature? Which are used in government documents, including legislation? Identify and distinguish among and between governments publications/legislation of the governments under study. By practitioners or in their organizations? What are the nuanced differences in these terms?

3. How is the terminology addressed in projects? What differences exist? Are there synonyms for benefits realization and benefits realization management in projects, programs, and portfolios?

4. How is the terminology used in portfolios, programs, and projects across the fields, such as academic research, consulting, government, practitioners, or their organizations? What differences exist?

The analysis phase of each literature review drew material relevant to the four questions in a systematic manner and the academic review used the following search terms:

- Benefits + Management,
- Benefits + Realis(z)ation + Management,
- Benefit + Management,
- Benefit + Realis(z)ation + Management

X3.1.2 FINDINGS AND REFLECTIONS FROM REPORT #1

Findings in the current literature (as of December 2016) highlighted the lack of common terminology in the definitions of benefit, benefits realization, and other related words (see Table X3-1).

Definitions of benefit in both research and standards suffer from a lack of consensus on whether the benefits should be (a) measurable, (b) the result a change, and/or (c) a way of demonstrating portfolio, program, or project contribution to organizational/strategic objectives.

Ambiguity and confusion around concepts make it less likely that BM/BRM will be successfully used in contributing to organizational objectives. This confirmed the need for a review of the terminology. Relevant literature showed a tendency to treat *benefits* as being synonymous with *value*. This has a number of dangers, illustrated in terms of differences between benefits maximization and optimization. Advantages and disadvantages of the use of *benefits management* and *benefits realization management* as alternative terms were provided and considered during the production of this practice guide.

X3.1.3 CONCLUSION AND RECOMMENDATIONS FROM REPORT #1

The report makes five main recommendations (see Table X3-2). Research and analysis of the unified view benefits management/benefits realization management to be integrated into PMI standards, highlighted characteristics leading to the conclusions and recommendations shown in Table X3-2.

Table X3-1. Summary of Report #1 Research Findings

Research Question	Report #1 Findings Summary
1. What is meant by benefits realization and benefits realization management?	Although the terms usually refer to a specific phase of a life cycle, this may lead to assumptions that benefits are only focused on the completion of a project or program. These terms need reinforcement to convey the need for active management processes to maintain a benefits' focus.
2. Are there synonyms for *benefits realization* and *benefits realization management*? Which of these are used in academic research, either in an empirical or conceptual manner? Which are used in the consulting literature? Which are used in government documents, including legislation? Identify and distinguish among and between publications/ legislation of the governments under study. Which are used by practitioners or in their organizations? What are the nuanced differences in these terms?	Several synonyms are used for terms and phrases in this context. *Benefit(s) management* can be used to mean both *benefits realization* and *benefits realization management*. Benefits management is a common term used by professional management bodies in their literature. Within government bodies, definitions focus on life cycle management, from the identification of benefits and realization planning to actual realization and review—including post-project or program closure. Many publications use this definition:[A] "The process of organizing and managing such that the potential benefits arising from the use of IS/IT are actually realized." Consultants and practitioners primarily use the term *benefits management*. *Value, value management* and other terms that include the word *value* have been used in various relevant literature. The term *value* has a close, but complex, relationship with *benefits*. In the literature of professional bodies, the terms *benefits* and *value* have three conceptualizations: (1) Value as a collective term for benefit or its equivalent, (2) *Value* as representing benefits, less the costs/resources required to realize them; and, (3) *Value* as a term representing the quantification of or other expressions of benefit. There are seven validated methods developed in the research of benefits, realization/benefits, management/ benefits, realization management, which could also be considered as synonyms for the management idea of benefits management/benefits realization management. There are also four invalidated methods, and six methods developed in practice.
3. How is the terminology addressed in projects? What differences exist? Are there synonyms for *benefits realization* and *benefits realization management* in portfolios, programs, and projects?	In both professional and government bodies of literature, the realization of benefits from programs and projects is mentioned from essentially two perspectives: (1) A view where benefits management activity is primarily at the program level—not the project level and (2) A view where benefits management applies to both the program and project levels. Academic literature complements the results of professional and government bodies of literatures, whereas for consultant/practitioners there is a diversity of opinions concerning positioning benefits in relation to projects, programs, and portfolios, sometimes diametrically opposed. Note—There is general consensus that a portfolio is a collection of programs and projects managed to achieve strategic objectives and programs.
4. How is the terminology used in portfolios, programs, and projects across the fields, such as academic research, consulting, government, practitioners, or their organizations? What differences exist?	The definitions of *benefit, benefits realization*, and *benefits realization management* do not display great variations between literature types. The conceptualization of benefits management and value/value management was not greatly differentiated, and the pattern of synonymous versus differentiated use also did not vary significantly. Academic literature has a greater focus on benefits at the project level. However, this is explained by the nature of academic contributions, often focusing on a project as a case study, and with a high proportion of sources concerned with IS/IT investments. A review of the terminology from professional and government bodies was addressed under two categories: (1) Initiative (program or project) level and documents; and (2) portfolio level for documentation and roles for benefits management/benefits realization management. Investigation into benefits management/benefits realization management suggests that there is a strong alignment in the types of documents and the terminology used for their titles in the roles in benefits management/benefits realization management.

[A] Ward, J. and Daniel, E.M. 2012. *Benefits Management: How to Increase the Business Value of Your IT Projects*, 2nd Edition. Chichester, U.K.: Wiley

Table X3-2. Report #1 Recommendations

	Report #1 Recommendations
1	This concerns the relationship between the term *benefits realization* and the umbrella term that applies to the management idea as a whole. There is a need for consistency in the usage of the terms *benefits realization management*, *benefits management*, and *benefits realization*. It is crucial to encourage the active management of benefits across and beyond the life cycle of the investment in change.
2	This concerns the relationship between *benefits* and value. The two concepts should not be regarded as synonyms. Focus should be on optimizing value as a relationship between benefits, costs/resources, and other areas such as risk.
3	This concerned benefits management/benefits realization management at different levels—portfolio, program, and projects and the wider organization. The recommendation is that roles at each level in benefits should be clear, and the processes for integration should ensure that people with responsibility at each level work together to optimize benefits.
4	This takes a wider focus, and concerns the wider organizational context. While benefits management/benefits realization management is a key part of the management of projects (including programs and portfolios, where applicable), responsibilities for benefits management/benefits realization management should extend across the organization as a whole.
5	Options should be explored to widen collaboration with professional bodies and academia across management disciplines. This should provide a wider perspective on the development of benefits management/benefits realization management and related themes.

X3.2 REPORT #2

X3.2.1 PURPOSE OF REPORT #2

Research report #2 was based on the following six questions:

1. What is the state of the art in measuring benefits?

2. At what point(s) in the project are outcome benefits measures developed, defined, and selected?

3. Who assesses the benefits and at what point during the project are they assessed?

    3a. Are measures added over the life of the project and/or beyond?

    3b. How far after the project closeout are benefits continued to be assessed, and at what intervals?

4. Does this vary by project type, for example, change project, innovation, or new product development, etc.? Or does this vary by industry, project size, potential social impact, or even who the customer is?

5. What kinds of measures are typically used to assess benefits, specifically quantitative and/or qualitative, and which are more frequently used? Does this vary by the same dimensions as Research Question #4?

6. What happens when there is a gap between benefits accountability and project implementation?

Table X3-3. Summary of Report #2 Research Findings

Research Question	Report #2 Findings Summary
1. What is the state of the art in measuring benefits?	The focus was on generic rather than specific approaches to benefits measurement with less on methods to measure them. Most of the government body sources are exclusively concerned with normative guidance, with some examples of descriptive information. Some sources were oriented specifically to portfolios, programs, or projects; however, a majority of sources were oriented towards programs and projects, and some publications were concerned with the integration between all three levels.
2. At what point(s) in the project are outcome benefit measures developed, defined, and selected?	A third of the sources did not address the question, but others agreed that pre-investment measurement is required. Only a quarter of the literature distinguished between outcomes/end benefits and intermediate benefits, using dualities (paired terms) such as intermediate/end, intermediate/ultimate leading/lagging and short term/long term. It was noted that the final benefits depend on intermediate benefits, but the reverse is not the case. Many benefits management sources emphasize the importance of the agreement of benefit measures with relevant stakeholders.
3. Who assesses the benefits and at what point during the project are they assessed?	Who measures the benefits is not always addressed (many address measurements but don't specify who should do it). Of those sources that did address this issue, most specified that it is a business responsibility, specifically: the business change manager and/or the benefit owner. Other sources highlighted the facilitating/coordinating role of PMO staff, specifically: (a) the portfolio benefits manager/benefits realization manager role; and (b) the benefits role in the portfolio/program/project office that collates and facilitates measurement by business managers or a similar role being performed by the program office. There were two main groups on the approach to assessment over the benefits life cycle: continuous or regular/periodic measurement and pre- and post-investment measurement.
3a. Are measures added over the life of the project and/or beyond?	This was not addressed by most of the sources, and those that did address this included identification and measurement of emergent/unplanned benefits. It was noted that cost/benefit and business case guidance focused on *planned benefits*, with little reference to *emergent benefits*. Emergent benefits are identified as (a) understanding how the investment is achieved, or (b) in response to changes to the internal or external organizational environment. There was only a small correlation with the use of benefits/value mapping techniques and/or lead and lag measures, indicating when such changes may be required.
3b. How far after project closeout are benefits continued to be assessed, and at what intervals?	This was not addressed by most of the references, but those that did noted the following: measurement continued after the program by benefits change manager/business-as-usual/operational managers and were accountable for benefits measurement following program closure.
4. Does this vary by project type, for example, change project, innovation, or new product development, etc.? Or does this vary by industry, project size, potential social impact, or even who the customer is?	Guidance was determined as being common across project type, industry, and size except for those directed towards e-government initiatives. The guidance was directed to (a) portfolio, program, and project practitioners and managers; (b) cross-sector global scope; (c) central/state/federal government, specifically self-regulatory organizations, (d) practitioners and business case writers; and (e) government initiative participants/policy makers. In general, there was little help in the research identifying variations in benefits measurement practice across different dimensions.
5. What kinds of measures are typically used to assess benefits, specifically quantitative and/or qualitative, and which are more frequently used? Does this vary by the same dimensions as Research Question #4?	Approximately 50 % of the literature sources did not distinguish between quantitative and qualitative benefits, with most focusing on quantitative measures. Sources referring to qualitative benefits/measures include those that see qualitative as providing less value than quantitative benefits/measures in contrast to those that recommended combining qualitative and quantitative benefits/measures. The key word in the description of measurement is relevant. Organizations often use large numbers of metrics and measurement, but the few key metrics that are relevant to creating and sustaining value are often lost in the noise. By definition, measurement involves quantification in some form.
6. What happens when there is a gap between benefits accountability and project implementation?	Literature on measurement/forecasting accuracy and benefits realization in practice also mentions the following: • Business cases do not always clearly identify expected benefits; when they do, business cases are commonly overstated due to optimism bias and strategic misrepresentation. This is one of the root causes of many subsequent failures of accountability; and • There is widespread and ongoing failure to measure benefits realization—particularly after delivery closure.

X3.2.2 CONCLUSION AND RECOMMENDATIONS FROM REPORT #2

The report makes eight main recommendations:

Research and analysis of benefit measurements, against the questions from X3.2.1, highlighted characteristics leading to the conclusions and recommendations outlined in Table X3-4.

Table X3-4. Report #2 Recommendations

	Report #2 Recommendations
1	More initiatives are needed to make evidence of benefits measurement management practice more accessible to BRM users.
2	Development of consistent and clear sets of terms for guidance on causal relationships involved in strategic alignment of delivery activity is needed. These terms should incorporate portfolio and program levels, where appropriate, to facilitate the benefits measurement process, especially in the area of direct use of benefits, as these can be used in dependencies/mapping tools.
3	Guidance is needed to build on progress toward owners of the BRM process and engagement with key stakeholders to develop benefits measures throughout the delivery life cycle. Useful tools include RACI frameworks and stakeholder workshops linking benefits to organizational priorities.
4	Guidance to emphasize the importance of benefits measurement and management over the whole life cycle, taking an emergent approach that stresses post-implementation benefits realization.
5	There is a need for the project, program, and portfolio management community to explore ways of encouraging an enterprise-wide culture of value, enabling potential benefits from investments in the change to be realized. Top to bottom organizational commitment to benefits identification and realization is essential, if potential long-term benefits are to be achieved.
6	Guidance is needed to establish a framework that allows different categories of investment and adoption of approaches to benefits measurement and management. This framework needs to embrace quantification and monetization, target setting, tracking and incorporating emergent benefits, maximizing long term commitments to measurement, and changes in behavior and attitudes towards the management of benefits.
7	Opportunities are needed to increase interdisciplinary collaboration with allied research should be promoted.
8	There is a need for increased efforts to address priority research gaps in the field of benefits measurement and management.

Both reports informed the PMI Standards Member Advisory Group, PMI Standards Manager and staff, and the committee that was chartered to develop this practice guide.

REFERENCES

[1] Project Management Institute. 2018. *Pulse of the Profession® Survey: Success in Disruptive Times—Expanding the Value Delivery Landscape to Address the High Cost of Low Performance.* Newtown Square, PA: PMI.

[2] Project Management Institute. 2017. *A Guide to the Project Management Body of Knowledge (PMBOK® Guide) –* Sixth Edition. Newtown Square, PA: PMI.

[3] Project Management Institute. 2011. *Practice Standard for Earned Value Management –* Second Edition. Newtown Square, PA: PMI.

[4] Project Management Institute. 2018. *The Standard for Organizational Project Management (OPM) –* Second Edition. Newtown Square, Newton Square, PA: PMI.

[5] Project Management Institute. 2016. *Governance for Portfolios, Programs, and Projects: A Practice Guide.* Newtown Square, PA: PMI.

[6] Project Management Institute. 2017. *Project Manager Competency Development Framework –* Third Edition. Newtown Square, PA: PMI.

[7] Project Management Institute. 2013. *Managing Change in Organizations: A Practice Guide.* Newtown Square, PA: PMI.

[8] Project Management Institute. 2017. *The PMI Guide to Business Analysis.* Newtown Square, PA: PMI.

[9] Project Management Institute. 2017. *The Standard for Portfolio Management –* Fourth Edition. Newtown Square, PA: PMI.

[10] Project Management Institute. 2017. *The Standard for Program Management –* Fourth Edition. Newtown Square, PA: PMI.

[11] Project Management Institute. 2016. *PMI Thought Leadership Series – Benefits Realization Management Framework.* Newtown Square, PA: PMI.

BIBLIOGRAPHY

This bibliography contains suggested reading for additional information on benefits realization management (BRM).

PMI PUBLICATIONS

Project Management Institute. 2016. *Pulse of the Profession® Report – Beyond the Project: Sustain Benefits to Optimize Business Value.* Newtown Square, PA: PMI.

Project Management Institute. 2016. *PMI Thought Leadership Series – Connecting Business Strategy and Project Management.* Newtown Square, PA: PMI.

Project Management Institute. 2016. *Pulse of the Profession® Report – Delivering Value: Focus on Benefits During Project Execution.* Newtown Square, PA: PMI.

Project Management Institute. 2016. *PMI Thought Leadership Series – Establishing Benefits Ownership and Accountability.* Newtown Square, PA: PMI.

Project Management Institute. 2016. *PMI's Pulse of the Profession® In-Depth Report: The Strategic Impact of Projects—Identify Benefits to Drive Business Results.* Newtown Square, PA: PMI.

Project Management Institute. 2016. PMI Thought Leadership Series – Strengthening benefits awareness in the C-suite; Newtown Square, PA: PMI.

OTHER STANDARDS AND GOVERNMENT PUBLICATIONS

Association for Project Management. 2012. *APM Body of Knowledge* – Sixth Edition. Buckinghamshire, UK: APM.

Australian Federal Government. 2012. *Assurance Review Process – Lessons Learned: Benefits Realisation Management.* Available from http://www.finance.gov.au/assurancereviews

Change Management Institute. 2013. *The Change Management Body of Knowledge* – First Edition. Sydney: CMI.

International Organization for Standardization. ISO 21504:2015 *Guidance on Portfolio Management*. Geneva: ISO.

International Organization for Standardization. ISO 21505:2017 *Project, Programme and Portfolio Management: Guidance on Governance*. Geneva: ISO.

State of New South Wales. 2015. *Benefits Realisation Management Framework Parts 1-5*. Available from: https://www.finance.nsw.gov.au/publication-and-resources/benefits-realisation-management-framework

UK Government. 2011. *Assurance of Benefits Realisation in Major Projects Supplementary guidance v1*, available at https://www.gov.uk/government/publications/assurance-of-benefits-realisation-in-major-projects

UK Government. 2017. *Guide for Effective Benefits Management in Major Projects*. Available from: https://www.gov.uk/government/publications/guide-for-effective-benefits-management-in-major-projects

OTHER PUBLICATIONS

Breese, R., Jenner, S., Serra, C. E. M., and Thorp, J. 2015. "Benefits Management: Lost or Found in Translation." *International Journal of Project Management*, *33*(7), 1438-1451.

Hellang, Ø., Flak, L.S., and Päivärinta, T. 2013. "Diverging Approaches to Benefits Realization from Public ICT Investments: A Study of Benefits Realization Methods in Norway." *Transforming Government: People, Process and Policy*, *7*(1), 93-108.

Jenner, S. 2014. *Managing Benefits: Optimizing the Return from Investments* – Second Edition. Norwich: TSO.

Jenner, S. (2010) *Transforming Government and Public Services – Realising Benefits through Project Portfolio Management*. Gower.

Kerzner, H. 2016. *Benefits Realization and Value Management*. Available from https://www.iil.com/resources/harold-kerzner-benefits-realization-and-value-management.html.

Letavec, C. 2014. *Strategic Benefits Realization: Optimizing Value through Programs, Portfolios and Organizational Change Management*. Plantation, FL: J. Ross Publishing.

Musawir, A. U., Serra, C. E. M., Zwikael, O., and Ali, I. 2017. "Project Governance, Benefit Management, and Project Success: Towards a Framework for Supporting Organizational Strategy Implementation." *International Journal of Project Management*, *35*(2017) 1658–1672

Renaard, L. 2016. "Essential Frameworks and Methodologies to Maximize the Value of IT." *ISACA Journal*, Vol 2.

Serra, C. E. M. 2016. *Benefits Realization Management: Strategic Value from Portfolios, Programs, and Projects.* Boca Raton, FL: CRC Press.

Terlizzi, M. A., and Albertin, A. L. 2017. "IT Benefits Management in Financial Institutions: Practices and Barriers." *International Journal of Project Management, 35*(5), 763-782.

Zwikael, O., Chih, Y., and Meredith, J. 2018. "Project Benefit Management: Setting Effective Target Benefits." *International Journal of Project Management, 36*(4), 650-658.

GLOSSARY

1. ACRONYMS

BAU   business as usual

BRM   benefits realization management

CSE   critical success enabler

OCM   organizational change management

2. DEFINITIONS

Anticipated Benefit. See *planned benefit.*

Benefit. A gain realized by the organization and beneficiaries through portfolio, program, or project outputs and resulting outcomes.

Benefit Categorization. A means by which a benefit can be identified and grouped for management in the organization.

Benefit Map. A graphical representation of the relationships of major elements needed to realize a benefit.

Benefit Owner. The individual or group accountable for direction, related decisions, realization, and sustainment of benefits throughout the organization's benefits realization management life cycle.

Benefit Profile. A description of the benefit, its intended beneficiaries, and criteria for its realization. This is a component of the benefits register.

Benefits Realization. The intended beneficiaries' integration of gains resulting from the use of outputs of portfolios programs and projects.

Benefits Realization Management (BRM). The day-to-day organization and management of the effort to achieve and sustain potential benefits arising from the investment in portfolios, programs, and projects.

Benefits Realization Management Framework (BRM Framework). A set of integrated governance and management practices designed to define, develop, realize, and sustain planned benefits.

Benefits Realization Management Life Cycle (BRM Life Cycle). The management of a benefit from conception through realization and sustainment, expressed in the generic stages of Identify, Execute, and Sustain. Also referred to as BRM life cycle.

Benefits Realization Management Plan. The planned activities, timeframes, and criteria for achieving one or more planned benefits or group of related benefits.

Benefits Realization Management Strategy (BRM Strategy). The organization's high-level direction for managing planned benefits achieved through portfolio, program, and project outputs and resulting outcomes.

Benefits Register. A repository in which benefit profiles are recorded. This may be used in aggregated ways at different levels of the organization to fit its needs.

Benefits Sustainment. The ongoing activities performed by the benefit owners and beneficiaries to ensure the continuation of outcomes and benefits achieved through portfolio, program, and project outputs.

Benefits Traceability Matrix. A grid that maps the planned benefits to portfolio, program, and project outputs. This is a component of a benefits realization management plan and may supplement the benefits register.

Direct Benefits. An unambiguous, measurable gain realized as planned by defined beneficiaries.

Disbenefit. A direct consequence of an output from a portfolio, program, or project that is perceived by one or more stakeholders as unfavorable.

Emergent Benefit. An unexpected benefit that arises during or after a program, a project, or within the context of a portfolio. Also known as *unplanned benefit* or *unanticipated benefit*.

Expected Benefit. See *planned benefit*.

Indirect Benefit. A secondary or incidental gain, planned or unplanned, realized by defined beneficiaries or by others, upon the realization of a direct benefit.

Intangible Benefit. A benefit that cannot be directly measured objectively and instead relies on a proxy or representative, measure, or evaluation.

Outcome. The results obtained through the use of portfolio, program, and project outputs.

Output. The expected deliverable of a portfolio, program, or project.

Planned Benefit. An intended gain for a designated beneficiary, selected and approved through the organization's benefits realization management system. Also known as *anticipated benefit* or *expected benefit*.

Tangible Benefit. A benefit that can be measured objectively based upon evidence.

Unanticipated Benefit. See *emergent benefit*.

Unplanned Benefit. See *emergent benefit*.

Value. The net result of realized benefits less the cost of achieving these benefits. The value may be tangible or intangible.

INDEX

A

Adapt benefits, 32
Anticipated benefit, definition of, 85
Assumptions of BRM framework, 25–26
Attributes of BRM culture, 16
Authorize charter, 28–29

B

BAU. *See* Business as usual
Benefit. *See also specific types of benefits*
    adaptation of, 32
    categorization of, 37–41
    definition of, 85
    examples of, 11
    as financial, 40–41
    identification of, 13
    as intangible, 44
    measurement of, 41–42, 45, 46
    quantification of, 33
    sponsorship and, 12
    sustainment of, 31–32
    as tangible, 43
    terminology and, 7
    types of, 38–41
Benefit categorization, 37–41
    definition of, 85
Benefit owner, definition of, 85
Benefit profile, 34
    definition of, 8
Benefits map
    definition of, 85
    example of, 36
    summary of, 35
Benefits realization, definition of, 86
Benefits realization management (BRM)
    CSE and, 14–19
    definition of, 86
    framework, 25–49
    guidance and, 51–52
    life cycle, 27–29
    need for, 2–4
    organizational context, 7–24
    plan concept for, 29
    portfolio roles and, 22
    principles and, 12–14
    program roles and, 23
    project roles and, 24, 55
    purpose of, 1–5
    organizational roles and responsibility in, 20–24

sphere of influence and roles in, 20
sponsorship and benefits, 12, 21
supporting tools for, 33–37
Benefits realization management framework (BRM framework), 25–49
definition of, 86
Benefits realization management life cycle (BRM life cycle), 27–29
definition of, 86
durations of, 52
measurement and evaluation in, 42
portfolio management and, 53
Benefits realization management plan
authorization of, 29
business strategy and, 10
concept of, 29
definition of, 86
development of, 28
elements of, 33
Benefits realization management strategy (BRM strategy)
alignment with, 15
definition of, 86
managing benefits and, 21
Benefits register
benefit profile and, 34
definition of, 86
example of, 55
identifying benefits and, 53
programs and, 23
summary of, 35
Benefits sustainment
concerns of, 31
definition of, 86
monitoring of, 31

Benefits traceability matrix
benefits and, 46–47
definition of, 86
example of, 37
mapping and, 49
summary of, 36
BRM. *See* Benefits realization management
BRM framework. *See* Benefits realization management framework
BRM life cycle. *See* Benefits realization management life cycle
BRM strategy. *See* Benefits realization management strategy
Business analysts, 28, 49
analysts for, 56
connections to, 10–11
objectives for, 47
Business as usual (BAU)
definition of, 85
organization changes and, 31
Business case
authorization of, 29
development of 28
Business strategy, 10

C

Categorization
benefit profile and, 34
of benefits, 37–41
Charters, 28–29
Critical success enabler (CSE)
of BRM, 14–19
definition of, 85
Culture, 15–16

D

Development
    of culture, 15–16
    of outputs, 30, 43
Delivery
    environment and, 18
    of outputs, 30
Direct benefits
    definition of, 86
    description of, 39
Disbenefit
    definition of, 86
    description of, 40
Documents, authorizing, 13

E

Emergent benefit
    awareness of, 55
    benefit category, 38
    definition of, 86
Enterprise program management offices (EPMO), 21
Evaluation method, 42
Execution, 27, 29–31, 54
Execute stage, 29–31
Executives, 4, 8, 27
Expected benefit
    categories of, 38–39
    definition of, 86
External/internal benefits, 41

F

Financial benefits, 40–41
Flexibility, 18–19

G

Goals, 9, 11–12
Governance
    framework and, 25
    resources and, 14
    risk and, 19
    roles and, 15, 16–17
Governance roles, 16–17
Guidance, 5, 51–53
    for practitioners, 1–2

H

Holistic planning and management, 14

I

Identification
    of benefit, 13
    stage of, 27–29, 54
    value drivers and, 48
Identify stage, 27–29
Indirect benefit
    definition of, 86
    description of, 39
Influence, 20
    factors and, 42–45
Information, 12, 34, 54
Insight, 15
Intangible benefit
    benefit category, 38
    definition of, 87
    example of, 44
Internal/external benefits, 41

L

Leadership, 17
   executives and, 4, 27
   organizations and, 47
Long–term/short–term benefits, 41

M

Management, 14, 25. *See also specific types of management*
   measures for, 43
   plan for, 33–37
   roles and, 17–18
Measurement
   of benefit, 41–42, 45, 46
   in BRM life cycle, 42
   examples of, 44
   factors and, 42–45
   management and, 43
   method of, 42
   timing of, 46

N

Need for BRM, 2–4

O

Objectives, 47
OCM. *See* Organizational change management
Opportunities, 28
Organizational change management (OCM)
   competitive advantage, 18
   acronym for, 85

Organizations, 21, 28
   benefits for, 11
   BRM and, 7–24
   considerations for, 48
   context of, 5
   framework and, 25
   leadership and, 47
   metrics for, 45
   performance of, 3
   resources for, 4
Outcome
   benefits tracking and, 19
   definition of, 87
   net benefits and, 13
   organizational strategy and, 9, 21
Output
   benefits tracking and, 19
   definition of, 87
   delivery of, 30, 52
   development of, 30–31, 52
   sustainment of, 31
Owners, 30–31
   authority of, 25
   Execution stage and, 29–30
   roles and responsibilities of, 15
   sustainability and, 31

P

Planned benefit
   awareness of, 55
   benefit category, 38
   definition of, 87

documents and, 13
tools and, 11
value drivers and, 48
PMO. *See* Program management offices
Portfolio manager guidance, 53
Portfolios, 10, 35
   BRM and, 22
   components for, 48
   context and, 26
   programs and, 51
Practices
   BRM life cycle and, 32–49
   BRM framework and, 25
Principles
   BRM and, 12–14
Profile, 34
Program management offices (PMO), 21
Program manager guidance, 54
Programs, 10, 26
   BRM and, 23
   portfolios and, 51
Project manager guidance, 55
Projects, 10
   BRM and, 24, 55
   context and, 26

R

RAM. *See* Responsibility assignment matrices
Resources, 13
   configuration of, 45
   governance and, 14
   measurement and, 45
   for practitioners, 4

Responsibility
   of executives, 8
   portfolios and, 22
   programs and, 23
   roles and, 15, 20–24
Responsibility assignment matrices (RAM), 20, 46
Risk, 19
Roles, 3, 56
   governance and, 16–18
   influence and, 20
   management and, 17–18
   of measurement, 46
   portfolios and, 22
   programs and, 23
   responsibility and, 15, 20–24
   of specialists, 18
   of stakeholders, 17

S

Short–term/long–term benefits, 41
Skill sets, 16–18
Specialist roles, 18
Sponsorship
   benefit and, 12
   strategy and, 21
Stakeholder roles, 37
Support, 53
   benefits and requirement traceability, 46–49
   benefits measurement, 41–46
   categorizing benefits, 37–41
   key interactions, 32–33
   supporting tools, 33–37

Supporting life cycle practices, 32–49
Sustainability, 27, 31–32, 33, 54–55
Sustain stage, 41–42

T

Tangible benefit
    benefit category, 38
    definition of, 87
    example of, 43
Techniques, 9
Timing for measurement, 46

U

Unanticipated benefit, 87
Unplanned benefit, 87

V

Value
    definition of, 87
    drivers for, 47–48
Visibility of roles, 15
Visualization of benefits, 39